Understanding Shari'a Finance

Understanding Shari'a Finance

Patrick Sookhdeo Ph.D., D.D.

Understanding Shari'a Finance

Published in the United States by Isaac Publishing
6729 Curran Street, McLean VA 22101

ISBN 978-0-9787141-7-8
Printed in the United States of America

Contents

Introduction

In the last two decades, there has been a spectacular growth in Islamic economics, including finance and banking. Originated and vigorously advocated by Islamist movements as a theoretical part of their ideology that Islam must dominate all areas of life, the Islamic economy has become a powerful force in the Muslim world and more recently in the West, developing new and sophisticated financial tools and forming a lucrative international market that cannot be ignored.

According to experts, the global market for Islamic financial products in 2008 was worth over £500 billion and it is expected to grow at 15-20% a year.[1] The Islamic Development Bank reported that by the end of 2006 assets managed by Islamic financial institutions were worth $800 billion.[2] Islamic financial products are likely to account for 50-60% of the total savings of the world's 1.2 billion Muslims within the next decade.[3] A McKinsey and Company study in 2007 estimated that the Islamic banking industry would grow 20% annually until 2012.[4] Already by the beginning of 2006 there were more than 300 institutions worldwide managing assets of $1 trillion in an Islamic way.[5]

Shari'a finance is a new phenomenon, which suggests that it is not in fact essential to the practice of shari'a. Shabir Randeree, managing director of the investment company DCD Group, who has completed several deals on "Islamic" principles, concedes this point: "I think it is fair to say that Sharia law was dead and buried for a long time."[6] It raises the question of why this kind of finance is now such a priority for many Muslims.

In fact, Islamic finance is part of the wave of Islamic resurgence and specifically part of the Islamist agenda.[7] This is stated repeatedly in Muslim sources. For example, Zamir Iqbal, a principal financial officer with the World Bank, and Abbas Mirakhor, an executive director at the International Monetary Fund, comment:

> It is important to remember that any Islamic economic system seeks consistency with Shari'ah not as an end in itself, but its ordering is part of a much larger unified whole.[8]

Shari'a finance is facilitated to a large extent by the vast amounts of money in the oil-exporting states, money which needs investment outlets. Western institutions and governments, eager to cash in on the growing Islamic financial market, have introduced Islamic finance and banking into the Western system, thus unknowingly encouraging the Islamist takeover of the Muslim world. The main goals of Islamic economics are political and religious, not financial, namely to gain support for radical Islam and to promote Muslim separatism. A growing concern for some observers is that the burgeoning world of Islamic finance offers terrorist *jihadi* groups a discreet way in which to raise and move the large amounts of money they need to maintain their activities.[9]

This book is written to raise certain issues of concern relating to the rapid progress of Islamic economics, internationally, in Muslim-majority countries, and in the West. It is not meant to be inflammatory, but to promote discussion of a subject that, although it has not yet made much impact on the public consciousness, is likely to become increasingly important.

History and Theology

Timur Kuran, a Muslim scholar and professor of Economics and Political Science at Duke University, claims that shari'a finance is an "invented tradition" of our times that does not go back to Muhammad's day. Even Islamic scholars of a century ago would have been very surprised at the modern version of Islamic economics.[10]

Islamic economics is a creation of the modern Islamist movements, who derive the concept from various verses in the Qur'an, from some frequently quoted *hadith*,[11] and from examples in the early days of Islam. It is because the Islamists interpret these sources according to a strict understanding of key terms, including *riba* (which will be discussed in the next chapter), that they have developed modern-day Islamic economics. In earlier centuries such rigid views about interest and profit do not appear to have been the norm.

Early Islamic Era

It is to be noted that Mecca was the site of a flourishing trading community, Muhammad himself was a trader, and religious texts, both pre-Islamic and Islamic, frequently refer to trade and to commerce. The practice of lending at interest was commonplace within pre-Islamic Arabian society, and many sources attest to its continued practice within the Islamic commercial system in most areas of the Muslim world up to Ottoman times. Nes'et Cagatay shows that despite what are deemed to be the prohibitions on lending at interest to be found in the Qur'an and *hadith*,

> Advancing money on interest had a long standing amongst all countries of the Faith. There are numerous examples of

transactions wherein both riba and interest were involved in Morocco, Algeria, Egypt, India, Iran and above all Mecca. Cahiz who lived in Basra in 9th century A.D. tells us in his Kitab al-Buhala about two Persian Gulf merchants who bought back for cash the same articles they has just sold on fixed term. Of the Abbasid caliphs Muqtadir borrowed some 200,000 dinars from merchants at a rate of interest of 7% between the years 912-932.[12]

Writing about what he terms "the conceptual openness of Islam towards business," Mustafa Akyol, a Turkish Muslim journalist who is opinion editor and columnist for *The Turkish Daily News*, attributes the decline of the Ottoman Empire to the decline in trade in the Muslim world (owing to the diversion of trade to Europe):

> The Islamic world was at the heart of global trade routes and Muslim traders took advantage of this quite successfully. They even laid the foundations of some aspects of modern banking: instead of carrying heavy and easily stolen gold, medieval Muslim traders used paper checks. This innovation in credit transfer would be emulated and transferred to Europe by the Crusaders, particularly the Knights Templar. So central was trade to Muslim civilization that its very decline may be attributed to changes in the pattern of global trade … The Ottoman Empire would excel for a few more centuries, but decline was inevitable.[13]

Aykol also demonstrates that the loss of trade caused by the shift in global trade from the Middle East and the Mediterranean, following the earlier depredations of the Mongols, created the conditions for the rise of religious bigotry:

> While the early commentators of the Koran cherished trade and wealth as God's bounties, late Medieval Islamic literature began to emphasize extreme asceticism.[14]

The Ottoman Empire

In the Ottoman Empire, lending and borrowing money, and obtaining loans against security that provided the creditor with considerable profit, took place from the early days of the Empire. There are many instances of charitable or pious foundations lending funds. The interpretations of the issues concerning *riba* have varied among the different schools of Islamic thought.

> There is evidence, for example, in the case of cash *waqf* (an interest-bearing trust fund) that its use was acceptable according to some interpretations of Hanifi [i.e. Hanafi] Fiqh, whereas it was unacceptable to the other schools. While this controversy continued in sixteenth century Ottoman Turkey, the actual practice of founding cash *waqfs* apparently was established in the fifteenth century, and by the seventeenth century it was generally accepted in the Ottoman legal and economic systems.[15]

Mehmet the Conqueror (1432-1481) used interest-derived income to help fund the Janissary army:

> The Conqueror was the first Sultan to set up foundations of which incomes – derived through loaning out on interest-rate – were used to meet imperial expenses. He had donated 24,000 gold pieces of which the interest was to be used to meet probable increases in the prices of the meat that was supplied to the Janissaries (the slave armies loyal to the Sultan).[16]

Ebusuud Effendi, the well-known Sheikh-ul Islam during the reign of Suleiman the Magnificent (1494-1566), granted permission for religious endowments *(waqfs)* to collect interest.[17] There was some controversy and a variety of *fatwas* written on the subject of *riba* and the permissibility of interest.[18] Some Islamic jurists "categorically prohibited the transaction of both articles and money even when what was involved was a low-rate interest."[19] Most, however, followed the permissive official line. In spite of some rigid interpretations of *riba*, in the Ottoman Empire

> Advancing and borrowing money amongst traders, artisans, public servants and the population in general was quite widespread, partly due to the special texture of communities comprising the Empire and because of the Imperial land system then in progress.[20]

A number of transactions given as examples in juridical texts demonstrate that interest was being charged but was being integrated into the sale value or price of the product. One judgment grants permission for a person who has advanced money on term at a rate of 15% to collect this *riba* at the end of the loan period.[21]

These documents – the *fiqh* and *fatwa* collections – and others such as registries and entries in the court of justice, attest to the fact that *riba*, understood as meaning a low rate of interest and not the repressive practices of usury, was widely accepted in the Ottoman Empire. The judgments made demonstrate that an interest rate of 15% was the accepted norm (although, interestingly, in Egypt the interest rate of 10% was commonly accepted in the nineteenth century). In 1609, Sultan Ahmet the First (1590–1617) ordered that money-lenders charging more than 15% interest be jailed and condemned to the galleys. These usurers would lend one gold coin and one kouroush (one gold piece was worth 120 aktchas and one kouroush 70-80 aktchas) on the rate of a monthly interest of four to five aktchas. They would earn 400-500 aktchas on 1000 aktchas loaned.[22] This appears to be equivalent to a rate of around 30% to 50%.

The practice of the State making advances to different bodies or individuals out of foundations set up by the State paved the way for the setting up of Foundations Administrations in Istanbul and Ankara at the inception of the Turkish republic in 1923. These eventually became the Foundations Bank, which was launched in 1954. The Ministry of Finance was created in 1838, and a banknote to replace the gold coin was issued in 1840. By the second half of the nineteenth century, the Ottomans officially legalized low rates of interest and the charging of interest in transactions of various kinds became official. In 1863 Midhad Pasha inaugurated a fund to advance credit to those on low incomes and paved the way for the first national Turkish Bank. Many banks sprang up and the interest accrued was spent on "public improvement." The example of the Ottoman Empire serves to demonstrate that the acceptance of the legitimacy of low-interest return on loans was widespread. Neither the firmans of the Caliph-Sultans, nor the *fatwas* of muftis and Sha al-Islamihs condemned it as *haram*. "Moreover," says Cagatay, "Mahmud Sheltut, the Rector of Cami al-Azhar in Cairo, published in 1960 an extensive study to the effect that neither today's bank rates nor shares nor saving bonds are haram."[23]

The Modern Era

At present, banking practices in general and practices on loan transactions regarding interest vary among Muslim countries, and it is this state of affairs that the Islamic resurgence seeks to address.

The drive for the establishment of an interest-free Islamic economic system was started by Abul A'la Mawdudi (1903-1979), founder of the militant Pakistani Islamist Jama'at-i Islami movement. Mawdudi argued that Islam encompasses all areas of human existence, including economics. Islamic economics was to be a vehicle to help establish Islamic rule and law in society and state.[24] The latter would be instituted in full when "the Ummah of Islam seizes state power."[25] This idea was further developed by his disciple, Khurshid Ahmad, a main leader in the Jama'at-i Islami in Pakistan and a prominent intellectual, politician, and economist, who helped transform Islamic economics into a contemporary academic discipline. The concept of an Islamic economy was integrated into the discourse of the Islamist struggle to weaken the West in preparation for the ultimate phase of establishing Muslim political hegemony in the world.

Hasan al-Banna, Founder of the Muslim Brotherhood, stated that the goal of Islam is to rule all of humanity all over the world:

> The Noble Qur'an appoints the Muslims as guardians over humanity in its minority, and grants them the right of suzerainty and dominion over the world in order to carry out this sublime commission … it is our duty to establish sovereignty over the world and to guide all of humanity to the sound precepts of Islam and to its teachings, without which mankind cannot attain happiness.[26]

Khurram Murad, a disciple of Mawdudi and a main leader in Jama'at-i Islami, wrote in his introduction to the English translation of Mawdudi's book *The Islamic Movement: Dynamics of Values, Power and Change*, which he edited:

> It is in the nature of iman [Islamic faith], then, that those who surrender themselves to God should strive to wrest control of all centres of power and authority from those in rebellion against God, not for themselves but to bring them under God … Therefore the "objective of the Islamic movement in this world, is revolution in leadership" at all levels and in all spheres of life … What is needed is organised, collective struggle – a Jihad to bring God's earth under God's rule.[27]

Isma'il al-Faruqi, the well-known Islamist scholar and professor of religion at Temple University in America, argued that Islam must pursue its political goal with all the power at its disposal to establish an Islamic world order:

> The Islamic state is ideological. It does have a world purpose which it pursues with all the power at its disposal. This purpose is the extension of itself to envelop the world ... The Islamic state is therefore not really a state but a world order, with a government, a court, a constitution and an army ... The Islamic state cannot rest until it succeeds in establishing this world order.[28]

Khurshid Ahmad explains that it is the task of the contemporary Islamic resurgence to reconstruct Islamic society, including its economy, in an integrated whole:

> Resurgent Islam represents a new approach – that is, to strive to reconstruct the economy and society in accordance with Islamic ideals and values and the needs of contemporary life.[29]

Ahmad also argues that Muslims must use Islamic economics to build up the power of Islam:

> It is a direct demand of *ummah's* position as *khalifah* that its dependence upon the non-Muslim world in all essentials must be changed to a state of economic independence, self-respect and gradual building-up of strength and power.[30]

In the note to this statement (note No. 31), Ahmad quotes Qur'an 8:61:

> Against them make ready your strength to the utmost of your power, including steeds of war, to strike terror into (the hearts of) the enemies of God and others besides whom you may not know.

This quote clearly reveals his real aim of using shari'a finance as a tool for the jihad against the non-Muslim world in the drive for Islamic hegemony. Jihad permits the plundering of the enemy's wealth.

Islamism thus aims at controlling the whole world and every sphere within it, including all economic systems and resources. Its goal is to implement a "new world order" under shari'a that encompasses all areas of life, including the economic. Its main enemy is the "crusading" West, which must be weakened and supplanted. Islamic economics must therefore be specifically Islamic and inherently different from non-Islamic systems, which they must endeavor to supplant.

Islamic economics became an efficient weapon in the hands of Islamists planning for Islam's domination of the world-system in all fields: political, military, economic and cultural. For them, the establishment of a worldwide universal Islamic state under shari'a is God's command to Muslims of all generations and the real aim of jihad. Islamic economics is but one of the many weapons in their arsenal.

Islamist states such as Iran, Sudan and Pakistan have forcibly Islamized their banking systems, and Malaysia is an enthusiastic supporter. Most other secular and semi-secular Muslim states did not see the need for it but tolerated shari'a finance in order to legitimate themselves in the eyes of their religious public. The Gulf States and Malaysia are spearheading the current move in favor of Islamic economics using the increasing power of their petrodollars.[31]

The Controversy
Over the Meaning of *Riba*

Islamist finance is defined by strict and literal interpretations of Islamic source texts on matters of trade and financial transactions. The main point of controversy has been over the interpretation of the Qur'anic prohibition of *riba*, as for example in Q 2:275

> Those who eat *Riba* will not stand (on the Day of Resurrection) except like the standing of a person beaten by *Shaitan* (Satan) leading him to insanity. That is because they say: "Trading is only like *Riba*," whereas Allah has permitted trading and forbidden *Riba*. So whoever receives an admonition from his Lord and stops eating *Riba*, shall not be punished for the past; his case is for Allah (to judge); but whoever returns (to *Riba*), such are the dwellers of the Fire – they will abide therein forever. [32]

Another often-used verse is Q 3:130:

> O you who believe! Eat not *Riba* doubled and multiplied, but fear Allah that you may be successful.[33]

The debate focuses on whether *riba* is considered to be interest or usury (i.e. extortionate and exploitative interest). The interpretation of *riba* as usury – thus permitting interest – allows Muslims to be easily accommodated in the global (Western-dominated) economic system. Interpreting *riba* as any kind of interest, however, demands the creation of a separate Islamic economic system, confusing for non-Muslims and dominated by Muslims. This is clearly in line with Islamist objectives of insulating the *umma* (the Islamic community) as far as possible from the non-Muslim world and of moving towards the Islamization of all world systems, including the economic.

Riba as Usury

Those who interpret *riba* as usury hold that what the Qur'an is banning is the pre-Islamic Arabian institution of *riba*, not modern interest, because the ancient *riba* system was very harsh and pushed defaulters into slavery. In seventh century Arabia, if a debtor was unable to repay a loan his debt would be doubled. If he defaulted again it was doubled again. This practice could soon lead to the debtor selling his house and all he owned, and eventually selling himself into slavery.[34] The banning of *riba* is seen as akin to modern bankruptcy law, a means by which a debtor unable to pay back his debt escapes the devastating results of the pre-Islamic system.[35]

According to this interpretation, limited moderate interest is allowed. Thus A. Yusuf Ali has translated *riba* as usury in his English translation of the Qur'an:[36]

> Those who devour usury will not stand except as stands one whom the Evil One by his touch hath driven to madness. That is because they say: "Trade is like usury," but God hath permitted trade and forbidden usury. Those who after receiving direction from their Lord, desist, shall be pardoned for the past; their case is for God (to judge); but those who repeat (the offence) are Companions of the Fire: they will abide therein (for ever). (Q 2:275)

In a footnote Ali comments on the controversy surround the definition of the word he translates as "usury" and offers his own definition as follows:

> Undue profit made, not in the way of legitimate trade, out of loans of gold and silver, and necessary articles of food, such as wheat, barley, dates, and salt (according to the list mentioned by the Holy Apostle himself). My definition would include profiteering of all kinds, but exclude some economic credit, the creature of modern banking and finance.[37]

Al-Azhar, the main Sunni center of religious studies, has argued that *riba* is usury or exorbitant and oppressive interest, and has proclaimed moderate fixed interest permissible. As a result most banks in Egypt pay fixed interest and the government issues interest-bearing bonds.[38] According to this view specifically Islamic financial institutions are superfluous.

In 1989, Muhammad Sayyid Tantawi, then Mufti of Egypt, issued a *fatwa* stating that interest paid by government bonds and ordinary savings accounts does not violate the spirit of Islam. He furthermore accused Islamic banks of hypocrisy and of misleading the public by using the word "Islamic" in their advertising, and claimed that Islam merely requires financial transactions to be characterized by clarity and justice.[39] In 2001, Tantawi's successor as Mufti, Sheikh Nasr Farid Wassel, declared that "there is no such thing as an Islamic and non-Islamic bank" and called for an end to the controversy about bank interest.[40] The current Grand Mufti, Ali Gom'a, recently reiterated the view that fixed bank interest is lawful under shari'a.[41] In October 2007, Tantawi (now Sheikh of Al-Azhar and President of its Islamic Research Academy) again asserted that predefined interest rates are lawful according to shari'a and do not count as unlawful usury.[42]

The Egyptian religious establishment is thus solidly against the Islamist version of interest as *riba*. The well known Pakistani reformer and scholar Fazlur Rahman took a stand similar to that of the Egyptian scholars in differentiating between interest and usury.[43] Likewise, Dr. Muhammad Saleem, an international banking executive, co-founder and former President and CEO of the Park Avenue Bank, N.A., New York City, says that

> An understanding of pre-Islamic and Islamic history and keeping in mind the context, would lead one to conclude that what the Quran bans is usury, not interest. Usury can be defined as interest above the legal or socially acceptable rate. Phrased differently usury is the exploitative, exorbitant interest rate.[44]

Riba as Interest

Modern Islamists have reinterpreted *riba* in the strictest possible sense to mean any interest whatsoever. They prohibit any kind of interest as anti-Islamic and anti-shari'a and claim that risk-sharing is the Islamic equivalent of fixed interest.[45] Islamists have transformed the various scattered shari'a injunctions on economic transactions into a comprehensive quasi-systematic economic system including detailed institutional and organizational procedures. Thus rather than going back to what was practiced in traditional Islam, they have created a different modern system. The well-known scholar Seyyed Vali Reza Nasr argues that in the past there was no all-encompassing Islamic body of economic thought, implying that the modern Islamic economy is a recent Islamist innovation.[46]

The Islamist position on interest is uncompromising; it has to be accepted as a matter of faith and no debate is permitted:

> The bottom line is that Muslims need no "proofs" before they reject the institution of interest: no human explanation for a divine injunction is necessary for them to accept a dictum, as they recognize the limits to human reasoning. No human mind can fathom a divine order; therefore it is a matter of faith (iman).[47]

The total ban on *riba* as interest means that it is not possible either to collect or pay interest on rented money as in conventional banking; for this reason shari'a finance developed as an asset-based system.[48]

Regimes in several Muslim states have adopted Islamic economics to appease Islamist groups, to gain legitimacy and to gain greater control of the economy.[49] Iran, Pakistan and Sudan have Islamized their banking systems by government decrees.[50] Malaysia, with its more traditionalist form of Islam nevertheless opted for the harsher Islamist interpretation of *riba*. Its Shariah Advisory Council (SAC) decided that:

> Upon close examination, the type of *riba qurudh* prohibited by Allah s.w.t. is similar to activities practiced by commercial banks and conventional finance companies. This is because banks or institutions give out loans and obtain interest from the loan.[51]

Malaysia went on to develop a large shari'a finance sector.

Additional Aspects
of an Islamic Economy

In addition to the elimination of interest, Islamists seek to set up a redistribution system based on *zakat* (the obligatory charitable donation which all Muslims should pay) operated by the government. In this model, governments will collect and distribute the 2.5% *zakat* tax. This is in effect a substitute for conventional income tax.

In October 2006, Saleh Kamel, chairman of the Islamic Chamber of Commerce and Industry in Saudi Arabia, announced plans to establish a World Zakat Fund that would streamline the collection and distribution of *zakat*.[52] The fund would operate on the basis of shari'a, and be run under the supervision of a committee made up of experts from the Organization of the Islamic Conference (OIC), the Islamic Development Bank, and the Chamber. It plans to have offices in every Islamic country and in others where large Muslim populations exist. Sheikh Yusuf Al-Qaradawi, chairman of the World Forum for Muslim Scholars, stated his approval of the proposed fund, saying that it would ensure the collection and distribution of *zakat* in a foolproof manner.[53]

The global concentration of *zakat* money could also have alarming implications for world peace. According to classical Islam, one of the causes in which *zakat* is to be used is the funding of jihad. This is based on the Qur'anic verse 9:60:

> Alms are for the poor and the needy, and those employed to administer the (funds); for those whose hearts have been (recently) reconciled (to Truth); for those in bondage and in debt; *in the cause of Allah*; and for the wayfarer: (thus is it) ordained by Allah, and Allah is full of knowledge and wisdom. – [Yusuf Ali translation]

The famous and authoritative medieval Qur'an commentary of Ibn Kathir (1301–1373) explains the term "in the cause of Allah" of this verse as follows:

> In the cause of Allah is exclusively for the benefit of the fighters in Jihad, who do not receive compensation from the Muslim Treasury.[54]

Sheikh Al-Qaradawi, discussing the matter of *zakat* and jihad in a BBC Panorama program in 2006 on "Faith, Hate and Charity," said,

> I don't like this word 'donations'. I like to call it Jihad with money, because God has ordered us to fight enemies with our lives and our money.[55]

Further aspects of an Islamic economy include the argument by Islamist scholars that shari'a prohibits trading in financial risk (*gharar*), as it is a form of gambling. They say that it is also forbidden to trade in alcohol, pork or any other commodities deemed *haram* by shari'a.[56] Islamists further maintain that the Islamic system demands a set of norms that ensures fairness and honesty in the market place.[57]

Muslim Critique
of Islamic Economics

Secular and liberal Muslims criticize Islamic economics and finance as being neither Islamic nor efficient. Some argue that Islamic banks conceal interest behind legal tricks, the interest simply being hidden and relabeled. Even some of the most notable supporters of Islamic economics, such as Professor Mahmoud A. El-Gamal, Professor of Economics and Statistics, holder of the Chair in Islamic Economics, Finance and Management at Rice University in Houston, Texas, and principal adviser and scholar-in-residence on Islamic finance at the US Department of Treasury, offer measured critiques. El-Gamal, who defines *riba* as all forms of interest, defines Islamic finance as:

> A prohibition-driven industry, which attempts to provide Muslims with permissible analogues of conventional financial services and products that are generally deemed impermissible in Islamic jurisprudence.[58]

However, he goes on to say that Islamic finance actually violates the spirit of shari'a and may facilitate the activities of criminal financial actors (see also page 42–43):

> Due to its emphasis on the forms of financial transactions rather than their substance, Islamic financial practices may violate the spirit of Islamic Law. Some peculiarities of asset-based Islamic financial products can make the industry vulnerable to abuse by money launderers and criminal financiers, who use similar methods to separate sources of money from its destinations. Hence, Shari'a arbitrage-based Islamic finance threatens to cause religious harm,

by subverting Islamic Law, as well as worldly harm, by exposing the industry to abuse and scandal.[59]

El-Gamal also argues that Islamic financial services, despite their rhetoric on avoiding interest, are in fact interest-based:

> Almost all contemporary writings in Islamic Law and/or Islamic finance proclaim that Islamic Law (Shari'a) forbids interest. This statement is paradoxical in light of the actual practices of Islamic financial providers over the past three decades. In fact, the bulk of Islamic financial practices normally base rates of return or costs of capital on a benchmark interest rate such as LIBOR, and would easily be classified by any MBA student as interest-based debt-finance.[60]

In his testimony to a US Senate Committee on Banking, Housing and Urban Affairs hearing on "Money Laundering and Terror Financing Issues in the Middle East," Dr. Mahmoud A. El-Gamal stated that, "Islamic finance was mainly envisioned by leaders of Islamist movements, such as Abu al-'A'la al-Mawdudí, Sayid Qutb, and Muhammad Baqir al-Sadr."[61] These are the same ideologists who invented the modern *Jihad fiqh* (the Islamic theology of jihad). Timur Kuran says of them, "As far as Mawdudi and his companions were concerned, Islam and the West could not coexist, and the two were locked in combat for the identity and loyalty of Muslims."[62] The implication is that the Islamist venture into creating a separate Islamic financial system was not inherently necessary for shari'a-observant Muslims, and had purely ideological motives.

Other critics accuse Islamists of misinterpreting the Qur'an and of ignoring real Muslim history, as well as using various ruses and legal fictions to maintain the appearance of the ban on interest. As no economic system can in reality function without interest, they argue, the Islamist system merely substitutes financial tools with other devices that are interest in disguised form to give an impression of compliance with their wrong interpretation of shari'a. Duplicity, however, is counterproductive, as any efficient economic system must be based on honesty and trust.[63]

Timur Kuran explains that the idea of Islamic economics was first floated by Mawdudi in the 1940s in his attempt to revive the Muslim *umma* and minimize its relations with the West. Kuran states that interest has not really been purged from Islamic transactions. All the complex invented Islamic financial tools involve thinly-disguised payments of interest. There is nothing really different about Islamic banks, and the concept merely serves the Islamist need to enhance Islamic identity and cohesion. Islamic economics have also dismally failed in relieving poverty in Muslim lands.[64]

Timur Kuran also argues that in countries where Islamic banks and conventional banks operate side by side, the returns on profits offered by the Islamic banks are almost identical to the interest-based returns of the conventional banks. He argues that this is evidence that Islamic banks, in spite of their rhetoric, actually realize their profits on interest-bearing investments and assets.[65]

In November 2006, Saleem Salam Ansari, who delivered the presidential speech at a seminar on Islamic Banking in Karachi, Pakistan, argued that the Muslim public is being exploited in the name of Islamic banking. He stated that the Islamic banking system in Pakistan was delivering huge returns for the bankers at the expense of the pious poor. The customers were losing on their savings, while the institutions were achieving returns of 22% and more annually. This was a "mockery" in the name of Islamic banking.[66]

Muhammad Saleem asks whether Islamic banks have achieved any of their original goals of making the economic system more "just, fair, equitable, and honest," and of promoting the economic development of the Islamic world. His answer:

> Sadly the answer is a resounding no. There is absolutely no evidence that the Islamic banks have made any contribution in either of these areas.[67]

Saleem describes all of the Shari'a financial tools and products as a "deception". [68] He contends that:

> An honest analysis of lending practices of Islamic banks would confirm that over 95% of the modes of financing employed by the banks entitle interest and that their practices only differ cosmetically from those of conventional banks." [69]

Further support for the view that the shari'a finance movement is not true to its own interpretation of shari'a has been provided by Sheikh

Muhammad Taki Usmani, chair of the Accounting and Auditing Organisation for Islamic Financial Institutions (AAOIFI), who declared in 2007 that 85% of *sukuk* (Islamic participation securities or bonds) were actually un-Islamic. After some debate, the organization issued a statement saying that any financial product with a buyback clause was un-Islamic because the risk-sharing aspect had been eliminated. It also said that products must be asset-backed, not merely asset-based.[70]

Sheikh Ahmad bin Mohammed Al Khalifa, the Governor of the Bahrain Monetary Agency, in his speech to a 2004 conference on Islamic Banking and Finance, described a major factor in the growth of shari'a finance. "Islamic banks," he stated, "have grown primarily by providing services to a captive market, people who will only deal with a financial institution that strictly adheres to Islamic principles"[71]

Summary

Islamic economics, then, provide financial support for Islamist organizations and parties that are seeking political dominance in Muslim states and in the world. They weaken the basis of secular regimes by restricting the economic, social and cultural interaction of Muslims with non-Muslims, while enhancing their own power base and expanding their influence in society. As the Islamic economy grows, other activities deemed un-Islamic are weakened, and government spending is redirected to Islamist causes. Successful Islamization of one sector tends to facilitate the Islamization of another in a domino-effect process. The growth of the Islamist alternative society with its myriad institutions is an important stage in the process of replacing secular with Islamist regimes.[72]

Islamist Triumph

At first Islamic economics were a theoretical exercise, but the oil wealth generated in the 1970s provided the means for implementing its ideals in practice.[73] Theoretical discussions soon gave place to practical ones on how to replace Western financial practices with Islamic alternatives.[74] Islamic economics has now taken deep root in countries such as Pakistan, Malaysia, the Gulf and Iran and is fast expanding in other Muslim states. Shari'a finance based on the principle of no interest has developed financial tools to suit the strict interpretations of shari'a by radicals.[75] Moving beyond the partnership-based financial tools, analogues to most Western financial products have been developed, including debt instruments and fixed-income investment vehicles.[76]

This new system attempts to encompass all Muslim wealth in the world as Islamists apply pressure on Muslim businessmen, Muslim governments and individuals to switch their wealth from Western banks and investment houses to Islamic institutions. One aim is to isolate Muslims and cause them to shun economic relations with non-Muslims, thus furthering the polarization deemed necessary for setting up the Islamist utopia.[77]

As Islamists of various streams become the dominant voice in Islamic discourse and gain political power, governments are giving in to their demands and encouraging the growth of Islamic economics.

The Organization of the Islamic Conference (OIC) established the Islamic Development Bank (IDB) in 1974 as an inter-governmental bank aimed at providing funds for development projects in member countries. The IDB provides fee-based financial services and profit-sharing financial assistance to member countries. The IDB operations are free of interest and are explicitly based on shari'a principles. In 1977, the OIC founded the International Association of Islamic Banks.[78] The AAOIFI was established in Algiers in 1990 and later moved to Bahrain. It issued its first set of standards in 1998.[79]

The First International Conference on Islamic Economics, under the auspices of the King Abdul Aziz University (Jedda), was held in Mecca in 1976. Over 200 delegates, mainly Muslim economists and *'ulama*, attended, including Khurshid Ahmad as one of its Vice-Presidents. This conference laid the groundwork for the Islamizing of economics. It made shari'a finance a respectable academic discipline and encouraged the establishment of the International Centre for Research into Islamic Economics at the King Abdul Aziz University. It also was the catalyst for the widespread teaching of Islamic economics in universities around the Muslim world and for research into this subject at institutions such as The Islamic Foundation in Leicester, The Council of Islamic Ideology in Islamabad, and the Pakistan Institute of Development Economics in Islamabad. Since then a growing number of conferences on Islamic economics have been organized in the Muslim world and more recently in the West.[80]

The interpretation that sees all interest as prohibited appears to have won the day, promoted by Islamist movements such as Jama'at-i-Islami and the Muslim Brotherhood. The Islamic economy has grown rapidly and has become a lucrative international market that cannot be ignored. As oil profits and other sources of Muslim wealth are recycled into Islamic investment products, the Islamic financial market will claim an ever-increasing share of the global market, while forcing Western institutions and states wanting to retain and increase their share in this lucrative market gradually to Islamize their own market systems.

As they do so, however, these financial institutions and states are arguably aiding their own long-term demise, and destroying the financial systems and the societies that allowed their function and success. Mohammed Al-Osaimi, the chairman of the shari'a group in Islamic banking in Saudi Arabia and professor of Islamic banking, claims that another effect is the development of shari'a finance in the West, and the competition thus created, which has forced many Muslim countries to take shari'a finance more seriously. He says that the most important reason for the flourishing of the Islamic finance system is that "international banks are convinced by the Islamic finance system, and this is manifested by their competition with the Islamic banks in the area of shari'a finance. This effort has forced local conventional banks in many Muslim countries to adopt the same system although some of them (the leaders of conventional Arabic banks) have not been convinced by it (Islamic banking)."[81]

The Islamic Fiqh Academy, a subsidiary of the Organization of the Islamic Conference (OIC), held a special meeting at Jedda, Saudi Arabia in December 1985 at which the assembled scholars declared that *riba* in any form was contrary to shari'a. This gave the signal for a large-scale development of Islamic banking and finance.[82] In a further Islamist twist, one of its decisions concerning what Muslims are permitted to do with interest accumulated in bank deposits stated:

> It is not permitted for the Muslim to leave the interest monies with the bank, since that would benefit the banks, especially if they are non-Muslim and foreign banks that may use such funds against Islam and Muslims directly or indirectly. This is being said with the full understanding that *continuing dealings with Riba-based banks, with or without interest, is not permitted.* [emphasis added].[83]

As Mahmoud Amin El-Gamal notes, "the same opinion was given earlier by the Fatwa Committee of Al-'Azhar in the 1960's with regards to deposits with foreign banks which were necessary to facilitate international trade."[84] Although conventional, non-Muslim banks may believe that providing shari'a-compliant financial products is firmly establishing them amongst Muslim consumers and expanding their business, which is not the case according to Islamic jurists.

Shari'a Finance as Jihad

In Islamic thought, fighting has two elements: the fighters and the money to buy weapons. This is asserted in many verses in Allah's book. "God hath purchased of the Believers their persons and their goods for theirs in return is the Garden of Paradise." [Qur'an 9:111] So the two elements of fighting are money and souls.[85]

The Islamist prohibition on interest is not merely a defensive and functional measure to excuse adherents from participation in conventional economies, but rather an antagonistic and strategic tool to replace and ultimately eradicate them.

The literal meaning of the word *jihad* is "to strive." Some Muslim scholars give three meanings in applying this term:

Jihad al-Nafs: ("soul"): that is, the personal struggle to avoid sin and adhere to Allah's commandment. It is called the greatest jihad because without engaging in *Jihad al-Nafs* a Muslim cannot advance to the next level.

Jihad bi'l-Lisan ("tongue"), *wa'l 'ilm* ("knowledge"), *wa'l qalam* ("pen"): that is, preaching, but also standing firm against the hypocrites, answering them especially when they attack the Muslim prophet Muhammad.

Jihad bi'l Mal ("wealth") and *bi' al-Nafs* ("self-sacrifice"): the struggle against the infidel and polytheists. In the majority of Qur'anic verses about jihad, the use of wealth in jihad comes first, before actual fighting and self-sacrifice. It is worth noting that self-sacrifice gains the highest reward.

A *hadith* narrated by Anas ibn Malik elucidates the third meaning:[86]

> The Prophet (pbuh) said: use your property, your persons and your tongues in striving against the polytheists. (Abu Dawud, 1033)

According to Qur'an and sunna, God commands Muslims to devote their wealth and their lives to jihad. Shari'a finance is a modern reconstruction and extension of the directives to economic jihad contained in the Quran and hadith. Shari'a-compliant finance is defined by its theological opposition to all non-Islamic forms of conventional banking, identified primarily by interest and risk. The financial products and operations of shari'a finance are based upon a mimicking or altering of these conventional financial norms, the results of which are deception and confusion.[87]

When the then-Malaysian prime minister, Mahathir Mohamed, founded the Islamic Financial Services Board (IFSB) in 2002, he stated, "A universal Islamic banking system is a *jihad* worth pursuing to abolish this slavery."[88]. *Al-Ahram's* report ("A Financial Jihad") explains that what he meant by "this slavery" is the Western "international monetary system that has driven many developing countries into the financial slavery associated with endless mountains of debt."[89] (It should be noted that as longtime prime minister, Mahathir led a Malaysian economy that grew over 10 per cent a year for nine consecutive years within the international monetary system.)[90]

Osama bin Laden spoke in similar terms about financial jihad, the guilt of *riba* (what modern Islamists deem "interest"), and the non-Islamic system's enslavement of others in his December 27, 2001 message:

> They shook America's throne and struck at the US economy in the heart. They struck the largest military power deep in the heart, thanks to Allah the Almighty. This is a clear proof that this international usurious, damnable economy – which America uses along with its military power to impose infidelity and humiliation on weak people – can easily collapse ... If their economy is destroyed, they will be busy with their own affairs rather than enslaving the weak peoples. It is very important to concentrate on hitting the US economy through all possible means.[91]

Some of the Islamic organizations, charities, and financial institutions that were involved in financing terrorism did adjust their methods and standards better to fit the new global requirements after September 11, 2001. To help shield and "stabilize" shari'a finance during this process and to begin to direct Muslim money away from conventional markets in the West, Muslim leaders created institutions such as the IFSB. As Zeti Akhtar Aziz, governor of the Central Bank of Malaysia, declared, "It is a legitimate objective to channel as much as possible of these funds into the Islamic world."[92]

It is evident that shari'a finance is considerably stronger than before September 11. The enormous capital that Islamic governments and individuals have accumulated through the quadrupling of oil prices has provided considerable economic and political leverage,[93] and it is an effective tool for increasing Islamisation, among Muslims first and in the world generally. Shari'a-compliant finance is, in effect, an economic jihad that succeeds in mobilizing Muslims who are not yet ready to participate in the fighting-type military jihad to share in jihad by other means.

Scriptural Sources for Jihad against Those who Participate in *Riba*

There are a number of Islamic source texts that pronounce God's curses and his wrath on those engaged in *riba* activities. In shari'a terms, this means such people are liable not only to punishment in the afterlife, but also to shari'a punishments in the present. It is important to consider a Qur'anic text that deals with the penalty or consequence of demanding *riba*.

> O ye who believe! Be afraid of Allah and give up what remains (due to you) from *Riba* (from now onward), if ye are (really) believers. And if you do not do it, then take a notice of war from Allah and His Messenger but if you repent, you shall have your capital sums. Deal not unjustly (by asking more than your capital sums), and you shall not be dealt with unjustly (by receiving less than your capital sums). Q 2:278-9 (Khan and Al-Hilali's translation)

The key phrase in this verse is the warning about "war from Allah and His Messenger" i.e. Muhammad. This would indicate a literal, violent jihad against those involved in *riba* activities. What do the traditional commentaries make of this verse, and how do modern Islamic religious jurists and scholars see it?

Ibn Kathir, in his commentary on these two verses,[94] refers to two *hadith* recording the words of Muhammad:

> There are seventy types of Riba, the least of which is equal to one having sexual intercourse with his mother." (ibn Maja 2:764)

> "May Allah Curse whoever consumes Riba, who ever pays Riba, the two who are witnesses to it, and the scribe who records it." (Muslim 3:1219)

Ibn Kathir then quotes from Al-Tabari's commentary (Muhammad ibn Jarir al-Tabari, 838-923, one of the most renowned of the early Muslim historians and Qur'an exegetes) on this part of the verse: "And if you do not do it, take notice of war from Allah and His Messenger", who wrote:

> Whoever kept dealing with Riba and did not refrain from it, then the Muslim leader should require him to repent. If he still does not refrain from Riba, the Muslim leader should cut off his head.[95]

Western governments, banks and others must recognize that Muslims who insist on shari'a finance believe that Allah's curse is upon everybody working in the non-Islamic banking system across the globe, and (according to Al-Tabari) that Muslim leaders have authority to behead those who persist in engaging in *riba* despite being warned.

It should be noted that this curse is directed not only against against Muslims but also against non-Muslims, as the Qur'anic verse and some of the *hadith* related to it also refer to Jews. The prominent contemporary Islamic scholar, Sheikh Yusuf Al-Qaradawi, quotes this verse in a section on "The Prohibition of Interest" in his 1994 book *The Lawful and the Prohibited in Islam (Al-Halal Wal Haram Fil Islam)*. Al-Qaradawi, Dean of the Shari'a College at the University of Qatar, author of over 20 books, and a regular preacher on Al-Jazeera and the BBC's Arabic website, states the following:

> At the same time, Islam blocks the way for anyone who tries to increase his capital through lending on usury or interest (*riba*), whether it is at a low or a high rate, reprimanding the Jews for taking usury, even though they had been prohibited to do so ... The Prophet (peace be on him) declared war on usury and those who deal in it; he pointed out its dangers to society, saying,

'When usury and fornication appear in a community, the people of that community render themselves deserving of the punishment of Allah'.[96]

Al-Qaradawi thus confirms that both God and Muhammad had declared war against those who practice the taking of interest. This means that they deserve a severe punishment in this world and in the next.

Dr. Mahmoud A. El-Gamal discusses the same Qur'anic text and various *hadith* about the prohibition of *riba*. He concludes:[97]

Any violation of the Hadith will result in one of two forms of forbidden *Riba*:

1. *Riba al-fadl*: where money is exchanged for money hand-to-hand, but in different quantities, or

2. *Riba al-nasi'ah*: where money is exchanged for money with deferment.

The latter form (*Riba al-nasi'ah*) is the one upon which most of western finance has been built. In the conventional financial sector, financial intermediation is effected through lending, and the time value of money is reflected in interest payments. As we have seen, this is unequivocal *Riba*, the devourer of which was warned of a war from Allah and His Apostle. Indeed, 'Abu Dawud narrated on the authority of Ibn Mas'ud (mAbpwh) said:

The Messenger of Allah (pbuh) cursed the one who devours *Riba*, the one who pays it, the one who witnesses it, and the one who documents it.

El-Gamal continues:

Similar traditions with slightly different language were narrated in Muslim, Al Bukhari, and Al Tirmidhi. Another most damning Hadith was narrated by Ibn Majah and Al Hakim on the authority of Ibn Mas'ud (mAbpwh) that the Prophet (pbuh) said:

There are seventy three different types of *Riba*, the least of which is equivalent [in sin] to committing incest, and the worst of which is equivalent [in sin] to destroying the honor of a Muslim.[98]

Citing such extreme *hadiths* puts enormous pressure not only on the Muslim community in the West but also on the government regulators in the US whom El-Gamal is advising on the development of policy. Every Muslim in the United States or elsewhere who has ever had a savings account, mortgage, or any other form of conventional banking is being encouraged to develop a deep sense of guilt, equal to the guilt he would feel had he committed adultery with his own mother!

Furthermore, Islamists are not only creating a moral prohibition against all forms of conventional banking but also giving a directive for the use of punishment, even capital punishment, against offenders. Establishing a new theological imperative for an Islamic financial system is not a minor or technical matter of separation from conventional banking, but the first step in a path that could lead to a call for its ultimate eradication and to violence against all involved in it. It is important that Western political leaders, economists and financial institutions, who have so quickly accepted and implemented an Islamic financial system (which they are told is shari'a-compliant), should understand the full implications and the possible consequences of their actions.

Financial Jihad as a Political and Economic Weapon

During the 1973 Arab-Israeli war, the Organization of Arab Petroleum Exporting countries (OAPEC), led by the Saudi king, decided to use their supply of oil to the West as a political weapon. When they temporarily stopped pumping oil to those states that supported Israel in the war, they discovered an effective means of political leverage, not only for the few weeks of war but for the following years.

The oil-exporting Arab states discovered the power of their wealth and the control they could exert over the United States and other countries. This initial booming of oil prices triggered the start of shari'a finance. The significant increase in the price of oil in recent years has produced an enormous flow of petrodollars to the Gulf countries. This has been of great benefit to shari'a finance and its manifold financial ventures. In addition, foreign conventional banks from across the globe have been drawn to do business on shari'a-compliant terms. Some conventional financial institutions provided new windows for shari'a finance, while others such as HSBC deepened their involvement, under programs such as HSBC/Amana Islamic banking.

In an invaluable study, "Oil and the New Economic Order," Gal Luft describes the significant structural changes occurring as a consequence of the rise in the price of oil:

> No doubt perpetual high oil prices will create a new economic world order, shifting the economic balance between OPEC and the West in the direction of those who own the precious commodity. Robert Zubrin points out that in 1972 the U.S. spent $4 billion for oil imports, an amount that equaled to 1.2% of our defense budget. In 2006, it paid $260 billion, which equals to half of our defense budget. Over the same period, Saudi oil revenues grew from $2.7 billion to $200 billion and with it their ability to fund radical Islam. In the years to come this economic imbalance will grow by leaps and bounds.[99]

The economic jihad is accomplishing what bin Laden described in his December 27, 2001 message:

> The economic bleeding is continuing to date, but it requires further strikes. The young people should make an effort to look for the key pillars of the US economy. The key pillars of the enemy should be struck, Allah willing. [100]

From where we stand now, in 2008, bin Laden appears to have misjudged only one thing: the need for "further strikes." With oil prices above $100/barrel, the size of shari'a finance has grown from less than $300 billion in 2003 to close to a trillion dollars in 2008. It may seem like a small percentage of the global economy, but with the still-rising demand for and price of oil, a weak dollar, enormous debts, and a credit crisis, the West faces something near to a hemorrhage in its economic strength and political power. "For America," writes Luft, "the perpetuation of the petroleum standard guarantees a metastasizing sovereignty loss, economic and political decline and eventual enslavement to OPEC and its whims."[101]

Deception and Confusion of the West as Part of Jihad

On almost every occasion that shari'a finance is mentioned in the Western media, in financial marketing products, in governmental papers and during hearings, it is described as a religious obligation based upon shari'a and its prohibition of interest. Yet in all of these contexts it is nearly impossible to find any discussion of the origins of shari'a finance, or of the debate over the definition of *riba*. Although journalists, bankers and officials confidently state the modern interpretation of Islamic law as prohibiting interest, there is rarely any mention of what it actually says. Whether this omission is the result of deception, corruption, apathy, fear, or ignorance, it is arguably the point of the West's greatest vulnerability in regard to shari'a finance.

To the founders of shari'a finance, the absolute rule of shari'a was not an individualized choice for Muslims, nor something limited to finance. "[It] is impossible for a Muslim to succeed in his aim of observing the Islamic pattern of life under the authority of a non-Islamic system of government," says Mawdudi.[102] "The objective of the Islamic Jihad is to eliminate the rule of an un-Islamic system, and establish in its place an Islamic system of state rule. Islam," he writes in *Jihad fi Sabilillah*, "does not intend to confine this rule to a single state or to a handful of countries. The aim of Islam is to bring about a universal revolution. Although in the initial stages it is incumbent upon members of the Party of Islam to carry out a revolution in the state system of the countries to which they belong, their ultimate objective is none other than a world revolution."[103]

Western financial institutions, journalists and government officials rarely take note of any of this debate.[104] Their assumption is that this is a religious obligation accepted by a consensus in Islam and therefore must be obeyed. This is bewildering and dangerous to all involved, not least for Muslims in the West who do not want shari'a finance.[105]

Malaysia, where a more traditional rather than Islamist form of Islam predominates, nevertheless opted for the harsher interpretation of *riba* and became a pioneer in developing its Islamic financial market. As early as 1995 its Shariah Advisory Council (SAC) decided that the securities of a company whose main activities are based on *riba* are not Islamically permitted and the company cannot be included in the index of shari'a-compliant companies.[106]

Western authorities have accepted Islamist interpretations of shari'a economic principles as representative of all of Islam. This has empowered Islamists, while weakening moderates and progressives. It has also placed individual Muslims under increasing communal pressure to use so-called shari'a-compliant financial products.

Tarek Fatah, a secular Muslim Canadian political activist, writer and TV host, made the following plea in a January 25, 2008 op-ed in the *Globe and Mail* newspaper:

> Many of us, who witnessed the medieval nature of manmade sharia laws in our countries of birth, heaved a sigh of relief back in September of 2005. We thought this was the end of the attempt by Islamists to sneak sharia into a Western jurisdiction. We were wrong. The campaign to introduce shariʻa is back. Last time, the campaign took a populist approach, invoking multiculturalism. This time, the pro-shariʻa lobby is dangling the carrot of new niche markets and has the backing of Canada's major banks. Such icons of the corporate world as Citibank NA, HSBC Holdings PLC, and Barclays PLC have endorsed shariʻa banking and have started offering Islamic financing products to a vulnerable Muslim population."[107]

Fatah is referring to the failed initiative to have Canadian civil courts enforce the decisions of Muslim shariʻa arbitration boards. His conclusion is that Islamists never take a break: having been defeated on one front they immediately launch a new attack aimed at furthering their goal of Islamizing Western society and bringing it under the sway of shariʻa.

We may conclude that shariʻa finance is part of a wider agenda of jihad, in accordance with the vision of Islamist ideologists of the overthrow of non-Islamic systems and the establishment of a pan-Islamic Caliphate that will rule the earth. One of their tools is deception, accomplished in part by mimicking conventional financial systems. The goal, as Mahathir Mohammed summarized it, is "a universal Islamic banking system."[108] In essence, it is the same ideology and dream of a global *umma* (Islamic nation) under Islamic law that is preached by Muslim extremists.

Dangers and
Vulnerabilities of Shari'a Finance

The dangers of the Islamic system of finance and banking lie in the objectives of its inventors, the ideologues of the Islamist movements. Their goals included the weakening of the West and Islamic dominion of all world systems: political, social, economic and cultural. This necessitates the destruction of the now-dominant Western systems and their gradual replacement by Islamist systems. Shari'a finance and banking are just part of the wider range of tools employed in pursuit of this goal. Western governments and institutions now gladly cashing in on the Islamic market are falling into the same trap into which Western governments fell when they supported Islamist radicals in fighting the Soviet Union. They are supporting the rise of a powerful system they cannot control and that might turn against them.

Islamist movements are at the forefront of the radicalization of the Muslim world and are fomenting the hatred for the West now popular in the Muslim street. They have created worldwide networks of linked organizations to further their goals. In the West, many of these linked groups appear outwardly moderate while secretly pushing for radical goals including the Islamization of Western societies. These movements include the Muslim Brotherhood; Saudi Wahhabi-Salafism; the Deoband movement and the Jama'at-i Islami. These have formed an international Islamist alliance that is everywhere agitating for Islamic states under shari'a and for the Islamisation of non-Muslim societies and states. Shari'a finance and banking is part of this drive.

Vulnerabilities of the Islamic Financial System to Fraud and Terrorism [109]

After the terrorist attack on the World Trade Center on September 11, 2001, the vulnerability of shari'a finance to unaccountable and illegal practices such as money laundering and the funding of terrorism became apparent. The United States and other governments sought to identify and break up financial networks connected to Al-Qaeda and related terrorist enterprises. Within a year of the attacks, the US had "blacklisted" almost 180 Islamic banks, associations, and charities as financiers of terrorism, including supposedly reputable institutions such as Al-Taqwa [piety] Islamic Bank, Dallah El-Baraka Group and El-Rashid Trust.[110]

Studies in recent years describe how the largest single source of funds for Islamic terrorism is *zakat* (the obligatory charitable donation for Muslims), which typically goes through the Islamic banking system.[111] Using the system of *zakat*, "al-Qaeda was able to receive between $300 million and $500 million" over a decade "from wealthy businessmen and bankers representing about 20% of the Saudi GNP, through a web of charities and companies acting as fronts, with the notable use of Islamic banking institutions."[112]

As we have already seen, Mahmoud El-Gamal realizes the vulnerabilities of shari'a finance to money laundering and terrorism:

> To the extent that Shari'a arbitrage Islamic financial practice utilizes the same tools as criminal finance, the industry may be vulnerable to abuse ... The current modus-operandi of Shari'a arbitrage Islamic financing is too dangerous ... The three stages of development of an Islamic financial product bear a striking resemblance to methods used by money launderers and terrorist financiers.[113]

Yet, the same year this paper was published (2005), El-Gamal said in his statement to a US Senate Committee hearing on "Money Laundering and Terror Financing Issues in the Middle East:"

> The conclusion of my analysis, as presented below, is that there is no reason – in theory – to suspect that Islamic finance would be particularly immune or particularly vulnerable to abuse by money launderers or terrorist financiers. In this regard, it is important to recognize that Islamic finance utilizes relatively sophisticated financial methods – originally devised for regulatory arbitrage

purposes – to synthesize modern financial practices from simple contracts such as leases and sales.[114]

This contradicts his views as expressed in the previous quote, and might stem from his desire to protect shari'a finance and the honor of Islam when presenting it to the government (maybe he is using *taqiyya*), in spite of his criticism of certain aspects of it when examining it professionally. As a pious Muslim, El-Gamal believes in shari'a finance, but he is critical of some of its present forms and practices, which he wishes to reform.

The fast rate of creation of Islamic financial products is outstripping the establishment of robust regulatory frameworks. Islamic banking regulations differ from country to country. Each country has a different approach to regulatory standards and to anti-money-laundering regulations. The Paris-based Financial Action Task Force (FATF), an inter-governmental body whose purpose is the development and promotion of national and international policies to combat money laundering and terrorist financing, has repeatedly expressed concern over this state of affairs. In Pakistan, for instance, accounting practices create ambiguous financial statements. Only limited companies are required to prepare periodic financial statements audited by a chartered accountant. International Islamic financial supervision structures lack effective enforcement powers to impose their standards across the board. This weakness could allow criminal exploitation of the system.

Because of the vagaries of the Islamic banking system, it is easier for Islamic institutions to conceal certain activities than it is for conventional banks to do so. Often, potential profits are undefined, making it easier for the transfer of illicit money through a pool of colluding depositors. Because there are no suitable financial instruments for short-term funding and Islamic banks cannot fall back on central banks as lenders of last resort, Islamic banks tend to transfer large amounts between themselves, so making themselves more attractive to potential money launderers. Islamic banks tend to pursue short-term investments to improve their profits, and this policy is also attractive to money-launderers. The custom of giving customers discretionary large-scale loyalty bonuses instead of fixed interest payments opens the door to possible illegal transfers.

Another source of grave concern is the interaction between tradition-al *hawala* dealers and the new Islamic banking system. (*Hawala* is an informal funds transfer system common in Islamic societies. It involves a huge network of money brokers located mainly in the Middle East and Asia.) Traditional *hawala* transfers are built on trust and do not leave a paper trail. *Hawala* dealers are now integrating with Islamic banks and using them as part of their transit networks. This practice again might enable illicit transfers and money laundering.

In Islamic insurance (*takaful*), company records are vulnerable to distortion and money can be hidden or lost through individu-als apparently receiving excessive payments. Payments must be made even if the premium payments were made with criminal monies. Company accounts are secret and are not regularly published, so they are open to falsification.

Some Muslim states have established offshore entities in order to attract foreign investment. In Bahrain, for example, 47% of the bank-ing institutions are offshore. These offshore holdings are vulnerable to money laundering as well.

The sovereign-wealth funds of some Middle Eastern countries have been hugely buoyed by oil revenues and the resulting liquidity. But set in the context of shari'a finance, such funds lack the transparen-cy necessary for effective monitoring and regulation by the interna-tional financial authorities. The sums of money are so significant that this deficiency has potentially serious consequences for the stability of world finance.

Efforts at Regulating the Shari'a Finance Sector

Shari'a finance has not yet succeeded in establishing regulatory standards of disclosure or transparency, and given its hostile opposition and non-conformity to conventional finance and its norms, it is unlikely to do so. There are many problems with financial systems such as shari'a finance that lack transparency or uniform standards, especially as most of them are operating within non-market or closed economies. Corruption is often the most persistent problem. Hence the urgent need for a global, binding, and strict regulatory system.

Shari'a finance is also facing problems that are rooted in the different practices across various countries and regions. Different shari'a interpretations in different regions lead to fragmentation. Screening criteria for establishing shari'a compliancy vary greatly. As a result, there are growing efforts globally to harmonize and standardize Islamic financial practices, mainly through the Accounting and Auditing Organization for Islamic Financial institutions (AAOIFI) and the Islamic Financial Services Board (IFSB). The goal is the creation of a worldwide network of Islamic financial markets.[115]

In November 2002, the Egyptian newspaper *Al-Ahram* reported on a historic gathering of Islamic banks from nine major countries to set up a "de facto Islamic central bank" in the form of the Islamic Financial Services Board (IFSB).[116] The IFSB was created to regulate globally institutions offering Islamic financial products. According to the main figure behind the launch of the IFSB, the Malaysian prime minister Dr. Mahathir Mohamed, the IFSB was established to respond to serious concerns about the vulnerability of shari'a finance to illegal practices such as the funding of terrorism, and "to absorb the 11 September shock and reinforce the stability of Islamic finance." Mahathir said in his speech:

It is a historic step aimed at internationalizing the Islamic banking and financial system. It will ensure that Islamic banking incorporates international best practices and standards for supervision and regulation. These must not only be consistent with Islamic principles, but also based on standards that are on a par with those observed in conventional banking.[117]

The article claimed that an Islamic financial system that

incorporates international best practices and standards for supervision and regulation was not the case before the advent of the IFSB, despite the best efforts of other powerful international Islamic institutions: Despite the establishment of the Islamic Development Bank (IDB) almost 30 years ago, and the AAOIFI[118] over a decade ago, a standardised regulatory authority for Islamic banking was sorely lacking until the advent of the IFSB.[119]

Whether the IFSB would be more successful as an international regulatory body was debatable from the start. According to the president of the Islamic Development Bank, Ahmed Mohamed Ali, "The IFSB's regulatory standards are non-binding so as not to encroach on the financial sovereignty of member countries." Building a regulatory authority to enact standards for accountability and transparency, however, was perhaps not the major concern of the IFSB. Six years later (in 2008), it is clear that the IFSB's other goal to "absorb the 11 September shock and reinforce the stability of Islamic finance" has been largely successful, driven by the petrodollar boom and Western banks' and governments' willingness to accommodate shari'a finance whether or not there are uniform, understood standards.

In spite of the tremendous growth in shari'a finance since the launch of the IFSB, a January 24, 2008 article in *al-Qabas* (Kuwait) about Islamic banks stated that "There are no globally accepted standards for shari'a rules."[120] Despite the huge growth, few financial or governmental institutions eager to tap into the growing stream of profits seem concerned as to why no international best practices and standards for supervision and regulation have yet been established.

In his speech at the 2004 IFSB Summit on the Islamic Financial Services Industry and the Global Regulatory Environment in London, Zeti Akhtar Aziz, the Governor of the Central Bank of Malaysia, said,

"It is imperative that the regulatory requirements need to be consistent with the injunctions of Shariah."[121] This reflects the *raison d'être* of shari'a finance: submission to the divine law expressed in shari'a.

If shari'a is the regulatory framework that defines Islamic finance, it would obviously not be willing to submit its workings to another regulatory framework, particularly one that is un-Islamic and is based upon interest (*riba*).

Aziz makes the claim:

> It is within this context of diversity of systems and players [shari'a finance and conventional finance] that the regulatory approach adopted needs to ensure harmonisation and a level playing field for a competitive and robust financial system ... The IFSB represents an important catalyst that will contribute to enhancing the resilience of Islamic financial institutions in the global financial system and that will strengthen the foundation for the progress in the development of the global Islamic financial landscape.[122]

What does Aziz mean when he speaks of the need to ensure harmonization? According to what standard or authority? Given the expressed directives of shari'a finance, the only possibility is a system "compliant" with shari'a.

The Role of Shari'a Experts
in Islamic Finance

The main institutions issuing *fatwas* on financial matters are the Fiqh Academy in Jeddah, Saudi Arabia, affiliated to the Organization of the Islamic Conference (OIC), the European Council for Fatwa and Research and the Fatwa Council of North America. These institutions are connected to the Islamist Wahhabi, Salafi, Muslim Brotherhood and Deobandi movements.

Shari'a finance needs three groups of specialists with complementary skills: [123]

- Financial professionals skilled in conventional financial products and knowing the needs of Muslim communities for Islamic products.
- Islamic jurists who can find precedents in classical Shari'a on which to base contemporary financial tools that comply with all possible Shari'a restrictions.
- Lawyers who can help both groups define and structure Islamic products while ensuring these comply with all relevant national and international legal and regulatory rules.

A group of specialist jurists in Islamic finance and shari'a has now emerged, who sit on a large number of shari'a boards of different banks and financial institutions, where they ascertain whether the financial products offered are shari'a-compliant.[124] Shari'a scholars are involved both in product development and in product approval. The earlier their involvement in the development stage, the easier the approval process will be.[125] Many of them also teach at Islamist academic institutions, and sit on the boards of Islamist organizations linked to the worldwide Islamist network. Bankers complain that there is a shortage of suitable shari'a scholars and that the price of a good *fatwa* is soaring as top scholars charge $10,000 per hour for their services and participate on the boards of up to 30 different institutions. It seems that it is not easy to find scholars with the combination of in-depth financial knowledge, shari'a expertise and knowledge of English. Most financial institutions thus draw their scholars from the same small pool.[126]

The shari'a board plays a central role in running Islamic finance. It is "one of the defining characteristics of an Islamic Bank" and what is called the "Legitimate Control Body". [127] The board is usually formed by a group of men who are qualified shari'a scholars with special expertise in the classical juridical pronouncements on economic activities. The shari'a board is an independent body employed by the bank and its views or *fatwas* are binding on the Board of Directors of the bank.[128]

The diversity of scholarly views is a serious challenge for conventional banks that run shari'a-compliant services. How far can a financial institution in the West be guided by a religious board basing its decisions on Islamic religious standards that are subject to alteration and to divergent interpretations from other scholars? One way that banks and financial institutions have tried to deal with this problem is to offer a multiplicity of shari'a lists that designate companies complying with shari'a regulations. But as *Asharq al-Awsat* (UK) reports in a March 12, 2008 article, this practice is troubling and confusing to many shareholders.[129]

The role of sheiks in making decisions creates many other problems that can destabilize the system. For example, the shari'a finance scholars at AAOIFI, which that sets standards across the Middle East, concluded that "about 85% of Gulf Islamic bonds do not really comply with Islamic law." After Sheikh Usmani, chairman of the AAOIFI, reported this judgment to Reuters in November 2007, it triggered huge concern across the Islamic financial world.[130]

Shari'a Lists for Trading

In order to certify financial firms as shari'a-compliant and worthy of investment and custom by pious Muslims, a variety of lists of companies dealing in Islamic banking and finance have been set up. These are set up by individual clerics, by Islamic financial institutions or by Western institutions offering Islamic products. They list two categories of shari'a-compliant banks and financial institutions. One group contains banks and companies that are considered fully "pure" and lawful (*halal*). The other group names institutions that are shari'a compliant but have some non-lawful activities or products, so they are "mixed". There have always been disputes between experts over the provisions of buying and selling shares. Some claim it is permissible to invest in companies with a percentage of interest-based activities. Others say it is totally forbidden. Others specify the upper limit of the unlawful share: some set it at 25% of total assets, others at 33%. The standards set differ between the various *fatwa* boards and institutions. The general guidance for Muslims confused by the multiplicity of lists is to follow the shari'a experts they most trust, "who are faithful and knowledgeable and who are not driven by whims or blind extremism."[131]

Although somewhat confusing, the implication of the logic driving this trend may be a reflection of the ultimate Islamist goal of the purification of all interest. But it is just as much a reflection of corruption, and an internal weakness within shari'a finance. The consequences are not only confusion, but manipulation, bribery and blackmail by the financial companies that are interested in attracting more funds.

These shari'a and half-shari'a lists and demands for "purification" of those institutions and capital involved in conventional banking may gradually pressure the global banks who have shari'a-compliant windows to move to full compliance with the Islamic law they have accepted and are in fact propagating. At the same time, as shari'a finance's share of the market grows, driven by the windfall of petro-dollars, which provides record profits and major returns, it is drawing more non-Muslim investors as well. Many are drawn by profit, while others may be attracted by the marketing of shari'a-compliant finance as more ethical, fair, and stable. When British banking giant HSBC Group began offering mortgages carefully formulated to meet Islamic banking practices last year in Malaysia, it was surprised that more than half of its customers were non-Muslim.[132] The goal is to sanitize the Islamic economy of conventional finance, yet open it to attract not only Muslim savings but non-Muslim money also. This is a further step toward the domination of shari'a finance over the global economy.

Impact of Shari'a Compliance

Many conventional banks and governments see enormous profits to be realized in shari'a finance, a system of "functionally equivalent" financial products based upon religious ideas that they presently find of little concern or relevance.[133] To Muslims, however, this divine directive is the preeminent point and the final say in the matter.

This adherence to the directives of shari'a above all other concerns or factors is evident in the decisions both of scholars and of ordinary Muslims, including those residing in the West.

Another example of the authoritative role that shari'a's religious doctrine holds in decision-making is evident in a matter related to the authorization of the Islamic Bank of Britain in 2004. According to the UK's Financial Services Authority (FSA) report, the main issue that arose concerned the definition of a "deposit".

In the United Kingdom, a deposit is defined as a "sum of money paid on terms under which it will be repaid either on demand or in circumstances agreed by parties". The point is important because deposit-takers are regulated and the customer is assured of full repayment as long as the bank remains solvent. *A savings account originally proposed by IBB as a "deposit" was a profit-and-loss sharing account, or Mudharaba, where Sharia law requires the customer to accept the risk of loss of original capital.* This was not consistent with the FSA's interpretation of the legal definition of a "deposit" which requires capital certainty.

After extensive discussions, the solution IBB adopted was to say that, legally, its depositors are entitled to full repayment, thus ensuring compliance with FSA requirements. However, customers had the right to turn down deposit protection after the event on religious grounds, and choose instead to be repaid under the Sharia-compliant risk sharing and loss bearing formula.[134] (emphasis added)

It is clear what their decision must be, even for those faithful Muslims whose deposits may be their only livelihood, and funds upon which they depend in daily life.[135]

According to Mohammed Ariff of the University of Malaya:

The bottom line is that Muslims need no "proofs" before they reject the institution of interest: no human explanation for a divine injunction is necessary for them to accept a dictum, as they recognize the limits to human reasoning. No human mind can fathom a divine order; therefore it is a matter of faith (*iman*).[136]

This may be the case for Muslims, but what reason is there for those Western, non-Muslim professionals in finance and government professions blindly to follow the dictates of shari'a finance?

Conclusion

Islamic scholars and some leaders are making strategic use of the impetuses of both faithful Muslims and Western financial institutions and governments to erect a massive and fast-growing parallel financial system based solely on religious fiat, and arbitrated only by themselves (Islamic scholars and ideologists). The effect of this is to segregate all Muslims from participation in any Western or non-shari'a-based systems, which they are working to subvert and ultimately to subjugate under the rule of Islam.

Islamists have been successful in creating an international Islamic economy to further their goals of insulating Muslims from non-Muslims, creating hostility between the two, and empowering their own drive for world dominion. However, contrary to their goals, the tendency is for the emerging Islamic economy to be driven by market forces and to become an integrated subdivision of the Western dominated global economy.

Essentially, shari'a finance is now producing approximations of Western financial practices. In this sense it simply reinvents accepted financial products and clothes them in an Islamic garb. It is not as yet a large proportion of global finance, and some commentators have highlighted various factors that may inhibit and limit its progress. Other observers believe that in due time most customers will realize that Islamic products are just copies of Western ones. On the other hand, shari'a finance has made considerable progress in recent years, and economic conditions (not least the current turbulence in conventional markets) may favor its continued growth, and may also increase the pressure for an Islamic currency to rival the dollar, the euro and sterling. As long as Islamism thrives and pious Muslims feel obliged to use it, its prospects are at least encouraging.

If shari'a finance does continue to develop, it may do so in three contexts: the world of international finance, where its presence is already very evident; the Islamic states, which are giving increasing support to its institutions (see Appendix 2 below); and among Muslim minorities in non-Muslim states. Regarding the last of these, the UK aspires to be the Western hub of shari'a finance, and the value of its Islamic assets is already among the ten highest in the world. The number of its Islamic investment banks is expected to more than double within five years, and the first "shari'a-compliant" MasterCard was launched in August 2008.[137] It is estimated that 2% of customers for some Islamic mortgages are non-Muslims who choose them for ethical reasons, because their funds are not invested in gambling, tobacco, alcohol or pornography.

Although shari'a finance and banking seem innocent and harmless ways of helping ordinary Muslims operate in a shari'a-compliant way in the economic arena, they have been created and promoted mainly by an international network of radical Islamist movements bent on furthering the world dominion of Islam. Their agenda is the establishment of Islamist states under Shari'a law all over the world. Islamic banking and finance is but one of the multiple tools they use to further their cause. It is economic jihad, a key and integrated part of the larger civilizational jihad.

In order to attract petrodollars many conventional Western banks have opted for short-term profits and opened shari'a-compliant financial windows, ignoring the long-term implications of these moves. On the other hand, Islamists have opted to intensify their push for domination and control of world finance. Both efforts are leading to the rapid Islamization of Western societies, as is now evident in the UK and other countries in Europe.

The response of governments and other authorities to this process requires urgent and sustained attention. Detailed recommendations cannot be provided here, but we suggest that it would at least be prudent for Western governments to exercise more discernment over their implicit or explicit support for shari'a finance, at least to the extent of recognizing some of its vulnerabilities and in particular its lack of external accountability. At a time of intense debate in Western countries over the proper role of religion in public life, the possibility of shari'a finance's giving to Islam an inappropriate influence over financial and economic policy must also be acknowledged. Political, economic and financial institutions are wise to take note of any possible threat to their own systems, and to provide necessary checks and balances before it takes effect. The provision of rigorous regulatory mechanisms for Islamic practices and products, according to internationally accepted norms, must therefore be a priority.

Appendix 1
Instruments of Shari'a Finance

The Islamic financial network operates with alternatives to interest such as profit-sharing with variable returns and shared risk-taking, as well as investments in assets. Investments are limited to products that do not invest in un-Islamic industries such as alcohol, pork, gambling, or pornography.[138] Islamic scholars have developed criteria to judge the shari'a-compliance of various financial products. Insurance posed a particular problem, as most scholars saw it as akin to gambling. They proposed an alternative, *takaful,* in which policy holders are viewed as contributors to a money pool which they agree to share in case of loss to any of them.[139]

The main principles of Islamic banking are:
- The giving or receiving of interest is forbidden. Shared profits replace interest.
- Money cannot be traded for money.
- Money can be used to buy goods and services which can then be sold at a profit.
- Money must be invested in shari'a-compliant ethical industries (no gambling, no pork, no alcohol, only *halal* foods, etc.).

Some of the main financial tools developed are:

Murabaha – sale at an agreed mark-up over seller's costs.

Ijara – leasing contract for a specified rent and term.

Usufruct – the legal right to use and derive profit or benefit from property that belongs to another person.

Mudaraba – profit-sharing partnership contracts where returns are calculated as a share of profits on ratio of investment.

Musharaka – joint venture, a form of equity participation contract in which bank and client contribute jointly to finance a project by issuing Islamic participation securities or bonds (*sukuk*).

Bay' al-Salam – payment in advance for deferred delivery of a commodity.

Bay' al-Sarf – rules on the exchange of money for money.

Bay' Mu'ajjal – deferred-payment sale.

Istisna'a – payment in advance for deferred delivery of a made-to-order item.

Bay' Bithamin 'Ajil (BBA) – a promise to buy by the customer to the finance provider.

Takaful – Islamic insurance based on pooling resources to help the needy.

Wadi'a – safekeeping of funds, interest-free current and savings accounts (bank may give discretionary bonus).

Qard hasan – "benevolent loan", i.e. interest free loan given to "needy people."

Joala – transactions based on a commission.

Tawarruq – loan using a three-party contract.

Appendix 2
Shari'a Finance in Muslim States

Several Islamic banks were founded in the 1970s in the Middle East. These included the Dubai Islamic Bank (1975), the Faisal Islamic Bank of Sudan (1977), the Faisal Islamic Bank of Egypt (1977), and the Bahrain Islamic Bank (1979). In the Philippines, the Philippine Amanah Bank (PAB) was established in 1973 by presidential decree as a specialized banking institution to serve the banking needs of the Muslim community. Its primary task was to assist rehabilitation and reconstruction in the Muslim south.[140]

At the core of the movement are two international groups: the Al-Baraka Group and the Dar al-Mal al-Islami Group (a holding company controlled by Prince Muhammad al-Faisal, son of the late King Faisal of Saudi Arabia).[141]

Large Western multinationals have opened Islamic windows for receiving deposits from wealthy Gulf state clients. These include Citibank, HSBC, Banque Nationale de Paris, and the Swiss UBS.

A problem facing state regulatory authorities is that it is difficult to make Islamic banks conform to the same liquidity and reserve requirements as conventional banks, which have access to short-term, fixed-interest funds.[142]

Interestingly, most governments in the Arab world were at first hostile or ambivalent to shari'a finance.[143] Only as Islamists gained in power and influence and as the Islamic resurgence developed did the new industry take hold. In some countries such as Libya and Morocco, Islamic banks are seen as being linked to Islamist political parties and are therefore refused banking licenses. In Egypt, Algeria and Tunisia, governments are extremely cautious in their approach to shari'a finance.[144]

According to Timur Kuran, the government-led Islamization of the economies in Sudan, Pakistan and Iran have all failed. Islamists blame the West and its corruptive influence for these failures, thus encouraging the violent elements in Islam to demand the elimination of all these sources of evil.[145]

Iran [146]

Iran imposed Islamic banking in August 1983 with the Interest-Free Banking Law of 1983 stipulating a three-year transition period. The law was implemented in March 1984, and banks were given 18 months to complete their conversion to Islamic banking principles.

The Interest-Free Banking Law prescribes that banks must set aside a portion of their resources for loans of the *qard hasan* type (benevolent loan). These are interest-free, but banks are allowed to recover expenses associated with granting them. Fees of 1.5% for institutions and 1% for individuals are common. The maximum tenure is usually five years for institutions and three years for individuals.

The Iranian system prohibits banks from paying fixed returns of any kind on current and savings deposits, but it permits the banks to offer incentives in the form of variable prizes or bonuses in cash or kind on these deposits. Banking fees may be waived and special services offered. The 1983 law is also vague on the remuneration of long-term investment deposits. Article 20 of the law gives the Central Bank the power to fix maximum and minimum percentages of profits that may be distributed to depositors.

The law specifies ten forms of financial instrument. The Central Bank of Iran has specified which types of financing are appropriate to certain types of transactions. For example, instalment sales and *qard hasan* are appropriate to finance personal consumption, while *mudaraba*, *musharaka*, and *joala* may be used for commercial finance. Term deposits (both short-term and long-term) earn a rate of return based on the bank's profits and on the deposit maturity.

Two private Islamic banks opened in Iran in 2001, and the Dubai Islamic bank opened an office in Tehran in 2002.[147]

Recent moves by the Ahmadinejad government and the Central Bank have caused some concern to Iranian banks. The new Central Bank governor, Tahmasb Mazheri, put forward a plan by which all profits on loans were to be eliminated. President Ahmadinejad called on bankers to offer cheap loans to people on low incomes, and to slash their profit rates to below the rate of inflation. In an economy plagued by high inflation this would mean banks incurring heavy losses and depositors being unwilling to put their money in the banks. As critics observe, banks cannot be expected to subsidize the poor – this is the duty of government.[148]

The Problem of Corruption in Iranian Shari'a Finance

The lack of transparency in several banking institutions led to some serious cases of corruption and fraud in the 1980s and 1990s. In response, the Economic Commission of the Iranian Parliament produced draft legislation in 2002 to combat corrupt practices and money-laundering offences.[149]

Islamic foundations, known as *bonyads*, reportedly account for 10% to 20% of Iran's GDP ($115 billion in 2002).[150] They are exempt from taxes, duties and most government regulation, and are formally under the oversight of only the Supreme Leader. In practice, they "answer only to Allah," and are "a law unto themselves."[151] These charities, says a Forbes magazine report, "serve as slush funds for the mullahs and their supporters."[152] It goes on to say:

> Many bonyads seem like rackets, extorting money from entrepreneurs. Besides the biggest national outfits, almost every Iranian town has its own bonyad, affiliated with local mullahs. "Many small businessmen complain that as soon as you start to make some money, the leading mullah will come to you and ask for a contribution to his local charity," says an opposition economist, who declines to give his name. "If you refuse, you will be accused of not being a good Muslim. Some witnesses will turn up to testify that they heard you insult the Prophet Mohammad, and you will be thrown in jail."[153]

Another report from a recent visitor to Iran concluded that "bureaucratic mismanagement and corruption is commonplace in the region. In Iran it is a far bigger obstacle to U.S. businesspeople than any reputed anti-American sentiment."[154]

Pakistan [155]

Although the well known Pakistani reformer and scholar Fazlur Rahman took a stand similar to that of the Egyptian scholars in differentiating between interest and usury,[156] the strong Islamist movements in Pakistan demanded an interest-free system, and achieved some steps towards it during President Zia's Islamization drive (1977-1988). From 1979, financial institutions were required progressively to Islamize their operations.[157] The move to Islamic banking in Pakistan was based on studies undertaken by the Council for Islamic Ideology (CII) which was responsible for much of the groundwork on the development of the financial system.

Recognizing the difficulties that could arise in transferring wholly to a profit-and-loss system without an adequate institutional arrangement or supportive environment, the CII suggested a three-year plan for the elimination of interest.

Interest was to be eliminated from bank operations, financial institutions, and other domestic financial transactions. During this phase, all national banks were to maintain a parallel system of profit-and-loss deposits, side by side with conventional accounts.

Islamic profit-and-loss accounts were introduced in 1981 in parallel with conventional accounts and banks were required to maintain separate arrangements for them. In 1985, the second stage was initiated, in which the banking system was supposed to operate all transactions on the basis of no interest, the only exceptions being foreign currency deposits, foreign loans, and government debts. The parallel system of Islamic and conventional banking was terminated. New deposits had to be on a non-interest basis and all financing had to be in Islamically-permissible instruments.

The Banking Control Department of the State Bank (Pakistan's central bank) is responsible for the rules governing the conduct of shari'a finance in Pakistan. In the early 1980s, the department issued a series of circulars defining in detail what types of finance could be used for which purposes, and what scale of fees could be charged.

In 1992, the Shari'a Court removed some important exemptions.[158] In an effort to stop the drive to a total Islamic economy, the Musharraf government asked the Supreme Court in 2002 to reconsider the question of interest-free banking and the powers of the Shari'a Court in its implementation. The government argued that what shari'a prohibits is the exploitative aspect of lending and that the correct translation of the Qur'anic word *riba* is usury, not interest.[159] However, in face of the growing demand for Islamic financial products, the State Bank of Pakistan established an Islamic Bank Department in September 2003 with the mission of facilitating the emergence of Islamic banking as the banking of first choice for providers and customers of financial services in Pakistan.[160] It also appointed a five-member Shari'a Board and posted a list of permissible Islamic banking contract forms on its website. By 2004 there were four Islamic banks, with two more in the pipeline, and 15 conventional banks had Islamic branches.[161] By 2007 there were six full-fledged Islamic banks with total assets of $2.6 billion, accounting for a market share of merely 3.4% in spite of the growth.[162]

In the desire to draw more investment from Islamic banks in the Gulf States, The Pakistani State Bank announced in January 2007 that it would launch Islamic treasury bills for the first time.[163] Middle East Islamic investors are now showing a growing interest in the Pakistani market.[164]

Sudan [165]

Sudan is the third Muslim state (after Iran and Pakistan) in which the whole banking system has been converted to shari'a finance by government decree.

The concept of Islamic banking was first introduced in the Sudan in 1977 with the establishment of the Faisal Bank (Sudan). Other Islamic banks followed.

Shari'a laws were implemented in Sudan in 1983, which included a requirement on banks to alter their business activities so as to be consistent with shari'a rules. In 1984, the whole banking system was transformed by presidential decree to work on an Islamic basis.

Owing to changes in governments over the period 1985-89, the process of Islamizing the banking system was interrupted several times. In 1990, the Central Bank fully implemented Islamic banking rules. All financial transactions must now be carried out using Islamic instruments conducted on the basis of profit-sharing and no fixed rate of return. Effective rates of return on bank lending are estimated and are not pre-fixed. On the liability side, banks are required to replace time deposits by investment deposits in which returns to depositors are fixed by principles of profit-sharing.

The Financial Institutions and Banks Act (1991), implemented in 1992, fixed heavy administrative and financial penalties for banks circumventing Islamic banking principles.

Malaysia [166]

Malaysia, where a more traditional rather than Islamist form of Islam predominates, nevertheless opted for the harsher interpretation of *riba* and became a pioneer in its development of an Islamic financial market. As early as 1995 its Shariah Advisory Council (SAC) decided that the securities of a company whose main activities are based on *riba* are not Islamically permitted and the company cannot be included in the index of shari'a-compliant companies.[167]

Official support for Islamic banking has been very strong in Malaysia.[168] As a result, Malaysia has positioned itself as an important center for shari'a finance and it developed one of the earliest mature shari'a finance markets. It tends to be more innovative than the more conservative Pakistani and Arab models.[169] It is home to the Islamic Financial Services Board (IFSB), a global organization of Muslim bankers in charge of banking regulation and supervision that works closely with the Bank for International Settlements. Islamic investments accounted for 11% of total banking assets in Malaysia in 2005. The Finance Minister predicted that by 2007, shari'a finance would grow to over 15% of total banking assets, and to 20% by 2010.[170] The Central Bank of Malaysia hopes to see Islamic deposits reach 10% of all bank deposits by 2010.[171]

The Islamic Banking Act of Malaysia, which was passed in 1983, provided the regulatory framework for Islamic banking practices. This was followed a year later by the Takafol Act, which covered the operations of Islamic insurance companies. The introduction of new Islamic financial regulations was not aimed at restricting the activities of existing conventional banks, but at providing a framework within which the new Islamic institutions could operate, such as the Bank Islam Malaysia Berhad (BIMB), which was founded in 1983 and by 2006 had mobilized some 2% of Malaysian sight and savings account deposits. Another exclusively Islamic bank is Bank Muamalat.

The Islamic Banking Act (1983) specifies four approved financial instruments – *mudaraba*, *murabaha*, *musharaka*, and *wadia*. No return may be paid on current accounts, although banks are allowed to give customers gifts.

The problem of Islamic banks' access to short-term funds was solved by passing a new Investment Act in 1983 under which the government undertook to issue short-term certificates paying dividends rather than interest.

In 2001 a new anti-money laundering law was enacted that abolished bank secrecy and provided for the overriding of client confidentiality. However, the penalties for offences remain comparatively lenient.[172]

A wide variety of Islamic financial products and instruments were introduced by the Bank Negara Malaysia (the Central Bank of Malaysia). In 1994, it created the separate Islamic inter-bank check-clearing system for Islamic banks. The clearing process and its regulations are based on the *mudaraba* principle.

The Bank Negara approved the founding of an Islamic Banking Center as the headquarters of the Arab-Malaysia Banking Group in 2001. The objective is to deepen the Islamic financial market and the co-operation between the Gulf region and Malaysia, strengthening Malaysia's position as a major center of shari'a finance.[173] Money will be transferred and advanced by banks in both regions for investment and loans to individuals and government-approved projects.

The Islamic market is well developed, and Islamic banking facilities are now offered by more than 23 banks and financial institutions. Contributory factors include the encouragement and support of the monetary authorities and the creativity of financial engineering in designing new products. Malaysia has pursued a dual banking system with conventional and Islamic banks existing side by side. It allows all banks to practice Islamic banking if certain terms and conditions are met: the first is to establish an interest-free banking unit at the parent bank; the second is to create and maintain an interest-free banking fund.

The Malaysian experience of Islamic banking has impacted neighboring countries. Indonesia established its first Islamic bank in 1992 (Bank Muamalat). Brunei created its first Islamic bank in 1993.

Saudi Arabia

Perhaps surprisingly, Saudi Arabia has been one of the last countries to allow Islamic banking, as its Monetary Authority was reluctant to introduce non-standard banking practices.[174] In 1975, the Islamic Development Bank was founded in Jeddah as an international financial aid institution under the auspices of the OIC. Its largest contributing states are Saudi Arabia (25%), Kuwait (12%), Libya (16%) and Turkey (8%).

Since 2004, Islamic banking has received stronger official support and the full spectrum of Islamic financing products is now available in Saudi Arabia. By 2005, more than 30% of bank assets in Saudi Arabia were classified as shari'a-compliant.[175] The Islamic Al-Rajihi Banking and Investment Corporation (ARABIC) has captured over 10% of the market.[176]

In 2005, Islamic banks in Saudi Arabia recorded massive profits.[177] In 2006, the financing of the huge $5.8 billion Petro-Rabigh project for high value petroleum products included $600 million of Islamic financing.[178]

A January 22, 2008 article on the *Al-Aswaq* website reported that by the end of 2007 Saudi Arabia had three fully Islamic banks, while another eight Saudi banks had a large percentage of daily transactions going through shari'a-compliant accounts, especially in personal banking. Another three banks (Alahli Alsaudi, Sab and Al-Riyadh) counted nearly 70% of their transactions as shari'a finance. Other financial institutions, such as investment funds, had about 90% of their transactions following Islamic banking regulations. Dr Muhammad al-Osaimi, an expert on shari'a finance, revealed that the Saudi regime is on the verge of enacting a new financial system that will lead to the Islamization of all the finance sectors in the country, including the Central Bank's "monetary agency".[179]

Gulf States

Gulf Corporation Council (GCC) states have an active Islamic banking component competing with the large sector of conventional banking. Islamic banks have become an important part of the banking system with significant market share and a clear niche role. Regulatory authorities in the various Gulf States have dealt in different ways with Islamic banks. In some of the smaller GCC countries, the Islamic sector has now captured some 20% of the market.[180]

Kuwait Finance House (KFH), founded in 1977, theoretically operates outside the control of the Central Bank of Kuwait. It does not have to conform to any reserve or liquidity requirements.

Bahrain has developed shari'a finance as part of its strategy to develop into a regional financial center.[181] Bahrain Islamic Bank was founded in 1979 by special decree.[182] In 1998, Bahrain established the ABC Islamic Bank. One of the largest Islamic banks in the region, Shamil Islamic Bank EC is based in Bahrain.[183] Al-Baraka Islamic Investment Bank and Maseaf Faisal al-Islami are both registered in Bahrain as exempt companies and hold offshore banking licenses. As of 2007, Bahrain hosted 34 out of 78 Islamic funds and had become an important target for large- scale Islamic investors.[184] In 2004, the Bahrain Financial Services Authority formulated the "Bahrain model" of Islamic financial standards to encourage the standardization of the operating practices of Islamic financial institutions.[185]

In the United Arab Emirates (UAE), considered a hub of shari'a finance, the number of Islamic banks has increased from one bank in 2000 to six banks in 2006, and it has increased rapidly from that time.[186] The Dubai Islamic Bank was founded in 1975, and there is also an Abu Dhabi Islamic Bank.[187]

In Qatar, the Qatar Islamic Bank was incorporated in 1982 and is now the fifth largest Islamic bank in the world.[188] The other Islamic bank in Qatar is the Qatar International Islamic Bank. The two Islamic banks account for some 12% of the total banking assets in Qatar.[189]

Oman is the only state in the Gulf that has not licensed Islamic banking. In February 2007, the executive president of the Central Bank of Oman, Hamood Sangour al-Zadjali, said that Oman would not allow Islamic banks because it believed banks should be universal, not specific.[190]

Traditional *hawala* transfers are very well developed in the Gulf States. Dubai especially has been a center for these discreet transactions, built on trust, that do not leave a paper trail. The amounts of money transferred by *hawala* have increased dramatically in recent years. *Hawala* dealers are now interacting with Islamic banks and using them as an integral part of their transit networks. This opens the door for illicit transfers and money laundering.[191]

India especially has expressed grave concern at the huge amounts of unaccounted-for money transactions to New Delhi and Bombay via *hawala* from the UAE. In response, the UAE Central Bank is now formulating a licensing system for *hawala* dealers in the Emirates.[192]

Jordan [193]

Jordan has a plural system which accommodates both Islamic and traditional banking. The Shari'a Law of 1978 provided for the establishment of Islamic banks, and the Jordan Islamic Bank was launched in 1978. In 1985 the Jordan Central Bank issued a ruling called the Jordan Islamic Bank (JIB) for Finance and Investment Law of 1985 which specifies the way the JIB could operate. The JIB has an extensive and relatively large branch network. Arab Bank has opened a new Islamic subsidiary, the Arab Islamic Bank.[194]

Shari'a finance has cornered some 10% of the market in Jordan.

Egypt

Since the time of the Egyptian reformist Muhammad 'Abduh (1849 –1905), Egypt's top religious establishment, which carries great weight around the Sunni world, has legitimated moderate interest in banking, interpreting the Qur'anic verses about interest (*riba*) by differentiating between permitted reasonable interest, and forbidden extortionate usury. Al-Azhar University, the main Sunni center of religious studies located in Cairo, has long argued for this reformist position that understands *riba* as usury or exorbitant and oppressive interest, and has proclaimed moderate fixed interest as permissible. As a result, in Egypt, most banks pay fixed interest and the government issues interest-bearing bonds. Indeed, in Egypt as many as nine banks out of ten pay a fixed rate of interest.[195]

In this view, specifically Islamic financial institutions are superfluous and questionable, especially as Egypt in the 1980s found itself in a financial crisis due to massive corruption flourishing in self-styled "Islamic companies." As we have seen, in 1989, the Mufti of Egypt, Muhammad Sayyid Tantawi, issued a *fatwa* stating that interest paid by government bonds and ordinary savings accounts do not violate the spirit of Islam. He accused Islamic banks of hypocrisy and of misleading the public by using the word "Islamic" in their advertising, and claimed that Islam simply requires financial transactions to be marked by clarity and justice.[196]

Tantawi's successor as *mufti*, Sheikh Nasr Farid Wassel, declared: "I will give you a final and decisive *fatwa*: so long as the banks invest the money in *halal*, then the transaction is *halal*." Wassel added that "there is no such thing as an Islamic and non-Islamic bank" and called for an end to the controversy about bank interest.[197]

In Egypt, Islamic banking peaked in 1986 and collapsed in 1987 when many Islamic investment companies went bankrupt owing to fraud and corruption. The Egyptian government has since encouraged conventional banks, led by the government-owned bank Misr, to open shari'a finance windows to mobilize deposits from pious Muslims.[198] Islamic banking remains rather limited, however.[199]

Turkey [200]

Turkey introduced licensing regulations for Islamic banks in 1983 and now has a dynamic Islamic bank sector. The regulations are contained in two communiqués, one from the Treasury and Foreign Trade Secretariat and the other from the Central Bank. The two communiqués provide specific guidelines for the operations of Islamic banks licensed as "Special Finance Houses" (SFHs) rather than banks.

SFHs are authorized to collect deposit funds from the public within Turkey and abroad, under special current accounts and profit-and-loss participation accounts. SFHs are required to deposit 10% of participation deposits and 20% of current deposits with the Central Bank as a reserve requirement. SFHs are permitted to offer current accounts or participation accounts. Current accounts receive no return and are not insured under the National Savings Account Insurance Fund. SFHs must retain liquidity ratios specified by the Central Bank. Fifty percent of the current account funds invested in commercial activities must have maturities of more than one year. Participation accounts must have a minimum balance specified by the Central Bank. They may have maturities of 90 days, 360 days or longer. The accounts are not covered by insurance. Their returns (or losses) are determined by the success of the ventures in which they are invested. The bank's share of profits or losses on investments is limited to 20% either way.

There are four SFHs in Turkey: Al-Baraka Turkish Finance House, the Faisal Finance Institution, the Kuwaiti Turkish Finance House, and the Anatolian Finance House. The Central Bank supervises the Islamic financial institutions in accordance with the decree that sets out the methods and procedures for the establishment of SFHs. It fixes the reserve and liquidity ratios, which differ from those of conventional banks. It audits the accounts and supervises the operations of the SFHs. The method of profit-and-loss distribution to SFH participation accounts is determined by the government.

The profit-and-loss participation deposit funds managed by SFHs are in the nature of an open-ended mutual fund. This feature of participation accounts has the potential of making participation account certificates a future capital-market instrument together with the creation of a secondary market in which these certificates are actively traded.

Three of the five private Turkish Islamic Finance houses are partly owned by the Al-Baraka Group, the Faisal Group and the Kuwait Finance House. Shari'a finance in Turkey reached a market share of approximately 4% by 2004.[201]

Syria

The government now promotes Islamic banking. In 2007, two Islamic banks were permitted to conduct Initial Public Offerings: The Cham Islamic Bank and the Syrian International Islamic Bank. At the Second Islamic Banking Conference held on March 13, 2007, Central Bank Governor Adib Maleh recommended that the Ministry of Islamic Trusts encourage Syrians to invest in Islamic banking and pay the *zakat* (religious tax) through Islamic banks. The government also licensed the first Islamic insurance company, Al Aqila, in March 2007.[202]

Indonesia

Islamic banks were recognized in Indonesia by law in 1992. This law was updated and amended in 1998. Bank Muamalat is the largest Islamic bank in Indonesia. Another large Islamic institution is Bank Mandiri. Indonesia finally passed anti-money laundering legislation in 2002. By 2006, Islamic banking constituted only 1.55% of all banking assets in Indonesia.[203]

Other

Islamic banks do not as yet exist in Libya or Morocco. They have only a small presence in the banking systems of Algeria, Lebanon and Tunisia.[204]

Appendix 3
Islamic Economics in the West:
Manipulating *Darura*

The European Council for Fatwa and Research, based in Dublin and linked to the Muslim Brotherhood and to Jama'at-i Islami, defined any bank interest as usury, declaring that it is a grave sin and forbidden.[205] The Council recommends that Muslims use Islamic alternatives. However, where this is not possible, it allows Muslims to buy houses using interest-based mortgages based on the shari'a rule that extreme necessity transforms the unlawful into lawful (*darura*). The Council also reminded Muslims of a traditional juristic principle accepted by most schools of law, which states that it is permissible for Muslims to trade with usury and other invalid contracts in non-Muslim countries.[206] This verdict shows that for most Muslims there was no theological necessity for implementing shari'a-compliant financial tools in non-Muslim countries. It is only the Islamist drive for creating autonomous Muslim spaces in non-Muslim states, as a step towards their Islamization, which can explain this deliberate interpretation of *riba* as forbidding all interest. Of course, once non-Muslim authorities grant these concessions, the argument from necessity disappears, and it becomes obligatory for Muslims to use these Islamic financial tools. This process leads to increased Islamization of the financial sector.

Shari'a finance first arose in the West to satisfy the demand of oil-rich Gulf investors who sought to invest their money in the West. Later, proponents of shari'a finance attempted to tap into the educated and professional middle class Muslim populations in the West.[207] The Islamic Banking System (now called Islamic Finance House), was founded in Luxembourg in 1978 as the first Islamic bank in the Western world. There is an Islamic Bank International of Denmark in Copenhagen, and an Islamic Investment Company has been set up in Melbourne,

Australia.[208] In 2006, the German Deutsche Bank opened an "Islamic Window" (a dedicated pool of money for Islamic business), separated from its other departments.[209]

Shari'a Finance in the US

Muslim residents began efforts to develop shari'a finance in the US in the 1980s. These were first focused on creating retail products, with some US banks offering shari'a-compliant savings and checking accounts as well as credit cards. Then came offers of mutual funds and financing for cars and homes. Significant efforts were undertaken to further shari'a finance in the 1990s when the Office of Comptroller of the Currency Administrator of National Banks (OCC) was asked by the New York office of the United Bank of Kuwait to permit Islamic residential finance products. The OCC responded via "Interpretive Letters" in December 1997 and November 1999, allowing new "functionally equivalent" arrangements.[210]

Most American states now allow residential *murabaha*, and many also allow commercial *murabaha*. Residential and commercial *ijara* products are allowed in some states, and pending in others.[211] In the new millennium, efforts to establish Islamic banks or credit unions have been consistently successful. National players include Guidance Residential, Lariba Finance House, Zayan Finance, Devon Bank, Amana Mutual Funds Trust and a few others.

Most Islamic financial activity comes from major international or foreign institutions serving themselves or non-US investors, mainly in the Gulf. Several Islamic investment banks have subsidiaries in the US.[212] Lariba Finance House, "the Oldest Community-Owned, Riba-Free and Shari'aa Compliant Finance" in the United States, for example, bases its models on the *fatwas* of Sheikh Yusuf Al-Qaradawi and Sheikh Muhammad Taqi Usmani.[213]

In June 2004, the US Treasury Department appointed Mahmoud A. El-Gamal as its principal adviser and scholar-in-residence on shari'a finance. The Treasury felt that with the growth in shari'a finance in the US, a deeper understanding of the issues concerned was a top priority.[214] As noted earlier, El-Gamal supports the proposition that *riba* in the Quran and *hadith* denotes all forms of interest.

The Saudi-funded Islamic Finance Project in Harvard Law School's Islamic Legal Studies Program has meanwhile facilitated much of the legal and shari'a scholarship in the field of shari'a finance and brought together, in one of its seminars, "the key players of Islamic financial institutions and regulatory agencies in the US government."[215] In April 2006, Dow Jones, Citigroup Corporate and Investment Bank launched a new Dow Jones Citigroup Sukuk Index, which measures their global performance in complying with Islamic investment rules.[216]

A test case for further Islamization took place in 2000 within the state of Minnesota. The branch office of the Council on American Islamic Relations (CAIR) undertook a campaign to press the county government (Hennepin County), the local branches of Fannie Mae (the Federal National Mortgage Association, FNMA), and the Department of Housing and Urban Development (HUD) to structure an "installment sales project where the county sold tax foreclosed houses" to Somali and other Muslims who were not willing to pay interest to buy houses in a subsidized lending program. Islamic scholars in Qatar and in the US reviewed and approved the contract. Although the effort was apparently unsuccessful in the end, the *American Journal of Islamic Finance* described its benefit in "bring(ing) Shari'a concepts and the needs of Muslim Americans" to the attention of "the highest level of the American mortgage industry and its regulators."[217]

Shari'a Finance in the UK

British Muslims, the British media, and the British government seem all to have accepted unquestioningly the Islamist interpretation of *riba* (i.e. the absolute prohibition of any kind of interest) and continually repeat the assertion that shari'a forbids the taking of any interest. There have been many calls in the press for the establishment of Islamic banks and financial institutions in the UK.[218] In December 2006, a BBC article stated as a basic premise, giving no conflicting Islamic views, that:

> Under Shari'a Islamic law, making money from money, such as charging interest, is usury and therefore not permitted.[219]

A number of articles appeared in the daily press expressing sympathy for the plight of Muslims who could not invest in Western stock markets, prospective Muslim house buyers who could not take out mortgages, and Muslim students who could not take out student loans, because they did not want to break shari'a rules.[220] The British

media have also persistently stressed the alleged ethical nature of
shari'a finance as opposed to the predatory nature of Western capital-
istic markets. Banks, eager to gain access both to UK Muslim finance
and to the international Muslim financial markets, joined the call for
shari'a finance. The HSBC, for instance, has claimed that:

> Conventional mortgages and current accounts are out of bounds
> for Britain's two million Muslims – the payment or receipt of
> interest is prohibited by Islamic law.[221]

However, in the very same article it admitted that some 70% of UK
Muslims homeowners have actually taken out conventional mortgages.[222]

The Bank of England established a working group to research the
problem, and in 2003 changed the rules on Stamp Duty to make
Islamic mortgages competitive.[223] In a shari'a-compliant mortgage, the
bank buys the house and rents it out to the buyer until he has paid off
the agreed-upon cost, at which time the house is registered in his name.
Under the former system the double registration first in the Bank's
name and later in the buyer's name would have meant paying Stamp
Duty twice, once at each registration. Under the new rules, Stamp
Duty is paid only once, making these Islamic alternatives cheaper and
more competitive. Treasury officials also indicated that there were no
longer any objections in principle to the introduction of shari'a-compliant financial products into the UK market.[224] In 2005, the government passed legislation to bring Islamic mortgages within the existing
conventional mortgage regime and to facilitate the creation of Islamic
financial transactions and retail bank services.[225]

In 2006, the Financial Services Authority (FSA) examined the possibility of issuing a regulatory framework to support the issuance of
Islamic bonds in London. This initiative followed the dramatic growth
in Islamic debt investment.[226] In June 2006, Stephen Timms, Chief
Secretary to the Treasury, stated that "Britain wants to support increasingly sophisticated Islamic finance and increased trade with Muslim
countries." The government, he said, was making good progress in
removing the legal and tax obstacles to the development of shari'a-
compliant financial products. London, he hoped, would become the
best base in the world for Islamic financial services providers.[227]

At the Islamic Finance and Trade Conference held in London in June
2006, the then Chancellor, Gordon Brown, declared that he wanted to

make Britain a center and gateway for shari'a finance.[228] Brown assured Muslim leaders that he wanted to create a level playing field for shari'a-compliant products in Britain. He hoped to make London the natural home for global Islamic funds, and to increase the inflow of investment from oil-rich Muslim states into Britain.[229] Brown also stated that London has more banks offering Islamic services than any other Western financial center. Ed Balls, then Economic Secretary to the Treasury, promised that the government would further act to remove any remaining tax barriers that impede the issuance of *sukuk* and the establishment of a secondary Islamic market in the UK. It seems that London has, indeed, become the largest center for shari'a finance outside the Muslim world.[230]

The efforts of the Treasury and of the Bank of England succeeded in creating a friendly atmosphere for shari'a finance in the UK, thus attracting needed investment. Following these official changes in policy, shari'a finance developed fast in Britain. British law firms such as Clifford Stance, Linklaters, Allen & Overy, and Norton Rose developed expertise in shari'a finance and made substantial inroads into the Islamic market.[231] The British Treasury Board welcomed the idea of starting an Islamic bank in the UK, arguing that having an Islamic financial market in London gives Britain an economic advantage. In 2004, the Islamic Bank of Britain was formed and mainstream banks hurried to develop Islamic expertise and provide suitable services. These include HSBC, West Bromwich Building Society, Barclays Bank and Yorkshire Building Society. All want a share of the huge market offered by Britain's approximately 2 million Muslims (including 5,000 millionaires).[232]

Lloyds TSB (UK) announced in June 2006 that it now offers Islamic financial services at every one of its 2,000 branches.[233] On 9 July 2007, the FSA authorized the launch of the Bank of London and The Middle East (BLME) as a standalone, wholesale, shari'a-compliant bank based in the City of London.[234] In January 2008, the Islamic Bank of Britain established its first dedicated Commercial Centre in London.

Most of the banks created internal shari'a supervisory committees (or councils or boards) to ensure that their products complied with a strict interpretation of shari'a, and they published the names of the scholars involved to reassure the Muslim community.[235] The HSBC Amanah Finance, for instance, is supervised by an independent "Shariah

Supervisory Committee," which regularly reviews its products and transactions to make sure they comply with shari'a. Three reputable Islamist scholars serve on this committee: Justice (Retd) Muhammad Taqi Usmani from Pakistan, Sheikh Nizam Yaqubi from Bahrain, and Dr. Mohamed Ali Elgari from Saudi Arabia.[236]

The British media have followed the trend by publishing numerous articles explaining the intricacies of shari'a finance to their UK audience. *The Times,* for example, published a special 16-page supplement on Islamic Banking on October 8, 2003.[237] It was full of praise for the ethical aspects of shari'a finance, describing it as a

> faith-based system of financial management that derives its ethos from Shari'a, the Islamic canon law ... Islamic banking is by far the largest of the ethical banking movements. One economist said it is one of the few original concepts to emerge from the South ... Contrary to popular misconceptions it is a universal concept open to all-comers ... The ethical principles of the financing system based on Islamic precepts are shared by the other two Abrahamic faith-based traditions, Christianity and Judaism.[238]

As of September 2007, the largest *sukuk*, a $3.5 billion issue by DP World, was written out of London. The European Islamic Investment Bank (EIIB) was established in 2006 as the first independent, wholly shari'a-compliant, Islamic investment bank. It is owned by a number of Gulf-based institutions and individuals. It located its headquarters in London and is regulated by the UK Financial Services Authority.[239]

By accepting Islamist interpretations of shari'a economic principles as representative of all of Islam, the British authorities have empowered Islamists, while weakening Muslim moderates and liberals. The latest developments have also placed individual Muslims under increasing communal pressure to use so-called shari'a-compliant financial products.

A Cautionary Note [240]

A warning note was sounded by a 2004 study on the demand for Islamic financial services in the UK. It claimed that most previous studies overestimated the demand for Islamic financial services in the UK. It found that 75% of the Muslim population in Britain was indifferent to shari'a finance and that there was no automatic demand for it.

It concluded that shari'a finance is "supply-led" and that those pushing for it and offering it will have to create the demand for it by attaching tangible benefits to Islamic products.

The study differentiated between three types of Muslim customers: staunch believers in the prohibition of interest, who would never use interest-based products (only 5%); "pent-up demanders," who consider both religious and other factors in choosing financial products; conventional customers who are reluctant to use shari'a finance, especially if it is more costly.

A quarter of British Muslims show an interest in shari'a finance but are happy using conventional services. Eighty-three percent of Muslims questioned the necessity of shari'a-compliant Islamic financial products approved by renowned Islamic scholars. More than 50% were unsure about how truly Islamic these services really were Only 17% accepted shari'a finance as broadly Islamic. Just 11% were satisfied with the Islamic financial products on offer in Britain, and barely 9% demonstrated a positive attitude towards Islamic mortgages.

Four factors were important in determining attitudes to shari'a finance: education, occupation, location, and income. Muslim professionals with higher education and income (a minority) are more likely to be interested in Islamic financial products than others. There is also a significant north-south divide: Muslims living in the north and Midlands (e.g. Manchester, Leicester) are much more interested in Islamic products than those in the south (e.g. London).

The study concludes that demand for Islamic financial services is not a purely religious phenomenon. This claim correlates with the assumption that shari'a finance is a politically-driven Islamist invention masked in religious idiom. It is clear that the Islamist movements have artificially generated the need and demand for shari'a finance. Another conclusion is that the support given by the government and financial sector to shari'a finance in Britain is aimed more at attracting investment from the huge pool of money in the oil-rich Middle East than in satisfying local Muslim demand, which is being used simply as a pious cover.

The UK Seen as the Most Shari'a-Friendly Financial Market in the West

A survey of several Islamic companies indicated that the UK was considered to have the most shari'a-friendly environment, in terms of human capital and expertise, institutional and legal frameworks, and political environment, of all Western countries.[241]

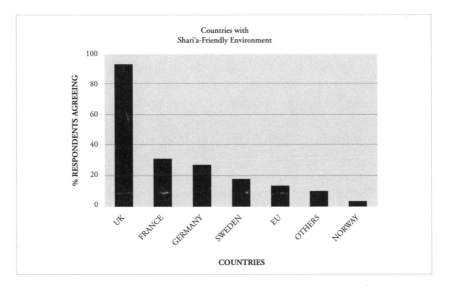

The UK is also the most favored European location for shari'a investors.

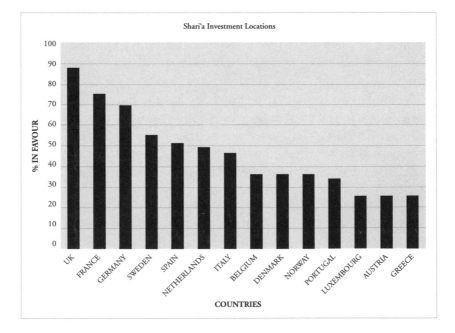

Institutions Involved in Shari'a Finance in the UK
- Barclays Bank
- HSBC Amanah Finance
- Institute of Islamic Banking and Insurance, Grosvenor Crescent, London
- Islamic Bank of Britain, Edgware Road, London
- West Bromwich Building Society
- Yorkshire Building Society

Individuals Involved in Shari'a Boards in the UK

HSBC Amanah Shariah Board

Justice Muhammad Taqi Usmani
Muhammad Taqi Usmani is a main leader in the Pakistani Deobandi movement. He has been a member of the Supreme Court of Pakistan since 1982. At present he is Vice President of Dar Al Uloom Karachi and Chairman of the Islamic Economy Center in Pakistan. Formerly, he was the Deputy Chairman of the Islamic Fiqh Academy, Jeddah.

Usmani is Chairman of the Shari'a Board of Accounting and Auditing Organization for Islamic Financial Institutions (AAOIFI). He is also Chairman of the Shari'a Supervisory Boards of Guidance Financial Group, USA; Saudi American Bank, Jeddah; and Citi Islamic Investment Bank, Bahrain; Vice Chairman of the Shari'ah Supervisory Board of Abu Dhabi Islamic Bank; and a member of the Shari'ah Supervisory Boards of Al-Baraka Group, Jeddah; First Islamic Investment Bank, Bahrain; and the Islamic Unit of the United Bank of Kuwait, among others. Justice Usmani holds Alimiyyah and Takhassus degrees from Darul Uloom, Karachi, an M.A. degree from Punjab University and an LLB from Karachi University.

Taqi Usmani also sits on the Shari'a Supervisory Board of the Dow Jones Islamic Markets Indexes.

Sheikh Nizam Yaqubi
Sheikh Nizam Yaqubi has contributed important original research on many aspects of modern shari'a finance, and is considered one of the world's leading experts in the field. He is a member of the shari'a supervisory boards for several Islamic financial institutions, including

Guidance Financial Group, City Islamic Investment Bank, and the Abu Dhabi Islamic Bank. Since 1976, he has taught *tafsir, hadith* and *fiqh* in Bahrain (institution not specified). Sheikh Yaqubi received his M.Sc. in Finance from McGill University in Montreal. He was educated in the classical shari'a sciences in his native Bahrain and in Mecca.

Sheikh Nizam sits on the Islamic supervisory boards of several Islamic financial institutions and is an active scholar in shari'a finance. He received a BA degree in Economics and Comparative Religion from McGill University, Canada. Sheikh Nizam is currently completing his PhD in Islamic law at University of Wales (United Kingdom). He works as an independent shari'a consultant based in Bahrain.

He is the author of several articles and publications on shari'a finance and other sciences in English and Arabic, including *Tahqiatul-A'mal fi Ikhraj Zakatil-Fitr bil-Mal, Risalah fit-Tawbah, Qurratul-'Aynayn fi Fada'il Birr al-Walidayn*, and *Irshad al-'Uqala' ila Hukm al-Qira'ah min al-Mus-haf fis-Salah*.

Yaqubi is shari'a advisor to HSBC Amanah, Abu Dhabi Islamic Bank, Bahrain Islamic Bank, Citi Islamic Investment Bank, and others. He also sits on the Shari'a Supervisory Board of the Dow Jones Islamic Markets Indexes.

Dr. Mohamed A. Elgari

As an established Islamic economist, Dr. Elgari teaches, writes and works with several institutions in the field. Dr. Elgari is the director of the Center for Research in Islamic Economics at King Abdulaziz University in Saudi Arabia, where he also serves as an Associate Professor of Islamic Economics. He is an expert at the Islamic Jurisprudence Academy, Jeddah. Dr. Elgari advises numerous Islamic financial institutions worldwide and is the author of significant research on the shari'a aspects of Islamic banking. He is shari'a advisor to HSBC Amanah, Bahrain Islamic Bank, Dow Jones Islamic Index, National Commercial Bank, Saudi American Bank, and the Saudi Fransi Bank. Dr. Elgari is a member of the Academic Committee at the Islamic Development Bank (IDB) and the Islamic Fiqh Academy in Jeddah. Dr. Elgari is also a professor of Islamic Banking at the Bahrain Institute of Banking and Finance and editor of the *Review of Islamic Economics*. Dr. Elgari received his Ph.D. in Economics from the University of California.

Dr. Muhammad Imran Ashraf Usmani

Dr. Usmani is a shari'a advisor to Guidance Financial Group, UBS-Warburg, Meezan Bank, Pakistan. He is a faculty member/teacher, has been teaching Islamic sciences for the past ten years in Jamia Darul Uloom Karachi, and has published several books and articles, including *A Guide to Islamic Finance* and *Meezanbank's Guide to Islamic Banking*.

Dr. Usmani holds B.A., M.Phil. and Ph.D. degrees in Islamic Economics from Karachi University. He also holds degrees of Alimiyyah and Takhassus (specialization in Islamic Jurisprudence) from Jamia Darul Uloom, Karachi. He has carried out extensive research in the area of shari'a finance, and has written several books on shari'a. Dr. Usmani is a faculty member/teacher of the Institute of Business Administration (IBA), Karachi. His book *Meezanbank's Guide to Islamic Banking* is well known in the industry. In addition to his academic activities, Dr. Usmani is a member of the shari'a committees of the following regulatory and financial institutions:

- State Bank of Pakistan
- HSBC Amanah, Dubai, UAE
- UBS Switzerland
- Mashreqbank, Dubai, UAE
- Guidance Financial Group, USA
- Hilal Financial Services, Dubai, UAE
- DCD Financial Group UK
- Future Growth Equity Fund, South Africa

Islamic Bank of Britain Shari'a Supervisory Committee[242]

Sheikh Dr Abdul Sattar Abu Ghuddah, chairman of the Islamic Bank of Briatin Shari'a Advisory Committee, holds a Ph.D. in Islamic Law from al-Azhar University. He taught at Imam al-Da'wa Institute, Riyadh, at the Religious Institute, Kuwait, and at the Shari'a College and Law Faculty, Kuwait University. He is Secretary General of the Unified Shari'a Supervisory Board of Dallah Albaraka Group, Jeddah. Ghuddah also sits on the shari'a supervisory board of the Dow Jones Islamic Market Indexes.

Mufti Abdul Kadir Barkatullah is imam of the North London Finchley Mosque. He acquired a Mufti (diploma) in Islamic law and a Bachelor of Islamic studies degree from the Islamic University, India. He also works as a supervisor at the Islamic helpline for Fatwa and as a presenter at Vectone Urdu.

Sheikh Nizam Yaqubi (for details see HSBC Amanah Shariah Board).

Lloyds TSB Shari'a Panel [243]

Sheikh Nizam Yaqubi (see above)
Dr Muhammad Imran Ashraf Usmani (see above)
Mufti Abdul Kadir Barkatullah (see above)
Mufti Muhammed Nurullah Shikder is a Barrister-at-Law and an imam at the Tunbridge Wells Mosque. He received a LLB degree from London Guildhall University. He advises individuals and businesses on shari'a finance.

Analysis of Individuals Involved in Shari'a Boards in the UK

These experts are linked to several Islamist movements and organizations that are at the forefront of the radicalization of the Muslim world and fomenters of the hatred of the West now popular in the Muslim street. These are the movements whose goal is the political domination of all states and societies in the world by Islam. Although the larger movements claim they are committed to legal methods to attain their goals, their ideology has spawned many radical groups and terrorist organizations. Saudi finance and the Afghan war against the Soviets have proved the catalysts for radicalizing these movements and transforming them into the dominant voice in mainstream Islam. They have supported first the *mujahidin* in Afghanistan, then movements in Kashmir, and later groups in various parts of the world where they feel Muslims are under attack. These movements have created worldwide networks of linked organizations and groups to further their goals. In the West, many of these linked groups appear outwardly moderate while secretly pushing for their radical goals and the Islamization of Western societies.

The movements with which these Islamic experts are linked include:

- The Muslim Brotherhood (founded in Egypt) and its worldwide network
- Saudi Wahhabi–Salafism and its worldwide network
- The Pakistani Deoband movement and its network
- Jama'at-i-Islami (based in Pakistan) and its network

These four Islamist movements have formed an international Islamist alliance that is everywhere secretly promoting Islamic states that are under shari'a and working for the Islamization of non-Muslim societies and states. Shari'a finance and banking is part of this drive.

The specialists in Islamic finance and shari'a dealt with in this report sit on a wide variety of boards and committees of financial institutions where they ascertain whether the financial products are Shari'a compliant. However, they also teach at Islamist academic institutions, and sit on the boards of Islamist organizations linked to the worldwide Islamist network.

Experts Linked to the Deobandi Movement

Justice Muhammad Taqi Usmani and his son, **Dr. Muhammad Imran Ashraf Usmani**, are both graduates of, and lecturers at, the Deobandi Dar Ul Uloom, Karachi. They both hold Alimiyyah and Takhassus degrees from this College, and Justice Muhammad Taqi Usmani is its vice-president.

Deoband is an Islamic reform movement in the Indian sub-continent started during the British Raj to combat the influence of Western civilization. Following the division of India and the creation of Pakistan, the Deobandi leaders committed themselves to the implementation of shari'a by the Pakistani state and founded Dar Ul Uloom Karachi, their Pakistani center, to further their vision. A Pakistani political party, Jami'iyatul 'Ulama-I-Islam (JUI) was founded to press for the necessary political and legal changes. Thousands of Deobandi *madrasas* (religious schools) were also founded to educate a new generation of committed youth bearing the Deoband message. These Deobandi *madrasas* were the seedbed of the Taliban movement, where thousands of Taliban jihad fighters were trained. JUI also has a military wing, which also provided the recruits for many of the terrorist organizations now active in Kashmir and Pakistan (Harakatul Ansar, Harakatul Mujahidin, Jaish-i-Muhammad, Sipah-i-Sahaba, Lashkar-i-Jhangvi). Its militant activities were supported and financed by the Pakistani Inter Intelligence Services (ISI) to serve Pakistani interests in Afghanistan and Kashmir. As late as April 2001, the ISI helped fund a Deoband conference in Peshawar at which delegates heard messages from the Taliban leader Mullah Muhammad Omar and from Osama bin Laden. Mawlana Fazlur Rahman, leader of the JUI, is fiercely anti-Western and especially anti-American, and he has threatened the US with jihad following the US-led invasions of Afghanistan and Iraq.

In his book, *Islam and Modernism*, Taqi Usmani asserts that an aggressive expansionist military jihad should be waged by Muslims against non-Muslim lands to establish the supremacy of Islam world-wide. He argues that Muslims should live peacefully in countries such as Britain, where they have the freedom to practice Islam, but only until they gain enough power to engage in battle. The book is a polemic against Islamic modernists who are accused of seeking to convert the Qur'an into a book of poetry and metaphor. He accuses them of being bewitched by Western culture and ideology.

His book aims to refute those who believe that only defensive jihad (fighting to defend a Muslim land that is under attack or occupation) is permissible in Islam. He also denies the suggestion that jihad is unlawful against a non-Muslim state that freely permits the preaching of Islam. Aggressive jihad was always commendable, he says, for establishing the glory of Islam, and there is no need to change this doctrine. Taqi Usman urged all Muslims to support the Taliban jihad. Taqi Usman was the religious mentor of the imam of the Red Mosque in Islamabad who, with his students, had to be overcome by the Pakistani security forces in July 2007 when they tried to implement shari'a by force and attacked other citizens. Usmani was a leading figure in the demand to declare Ahmadis non-Muslim in Pakistan. He supported the Afghan jihad in the 1980s, claiming that it was a religious practice equivalent to the pilgrimage.

Experts Linked to Wahhabism

These are represented by Shaykh Nizam Yaqubi and Dr. Mohamed A. Elgari, both of whom have links with Saudi Arabia, as we have seen above.

Saudi Arabia is the center of Wahhabi Islam, a movement that started as a marginal radical reform group that treated other Muslims as heretics and apostates who should be forced into the true faith or killed. The oil riches flowing into the Saudi coffers, especially since the 1970s, have enabled Wahhabi Islam to become a dominant force, as it created alliances with other Islamist movements, especially the Muslim Brotherhood, Jama'at-i-Islami, and Deoband, and subverted other groups by generous provision of funds. Saudi-sponsored Muslim umbrella organizations have consistently pushed for the Islamization of Muslim states, the Islamization of Western societies, and the expansion of radical Islam into non-Muslim areas. The Islamic Fiqh Academy in Jeddah, where Dr Elgari is an member, is a subsidiary of the Organization of the Islamic Conference (OIC), and its aim is to lay the foundation for shari'a to be implemented in all Muslim societies and states, as well as to increase its influence in non-Muslim societies and in the international arena.

Experts Linked to Jama'at-i-Islami and the Muslim Brotherhood

Justice Muhammad Taqi Usmani and Sheikh Nizam Yaqubi are Islamic financial experts with links to Jama'at-i-Islami and the Muslim Brotherhood. They serve on the International Advisory Council of the Markfield Institute of Higher Education, a subsidiary of the Islamic Foundation in Leicester, UK. These institutions are part of the world-wide Jama'at-i Islami network. In Pakistan, Jama'at-i Islami is a hard-line Islamist movement and political party dedicated to the formation of an Islamic state under shari'a in Pakistan, as well as in all Muslim states and eventually in all societies and states in the world. Its branches in the UK and the West tend to present a moderate face while advancing the Islamist agenda. In Pakistan it successfully agitated for the state to declare the Ahmadiyya movement as non-Islamic, provided the ideological underpinning for the Islamization of the Pakistani legal system under President Zia-ul Haq and created its own *mujahidin* groups to fight in Afghanistan and Kashmir.

Sheikh Yusuf al-Qaradawi, a main spiritual leader of the Muslim Brotherhood who now lives in Qatar, sits on the same International Advisory Council. The Muslim Brotherhood is illegal in Egypt, where the government is suspicious of its popularity, power, and ability to destabilize the regime. Like the other movements, it is dedicated to the founding of Islamic states under shari'a everywhere. Although it claims to be non-violent, it supports Hamas and sent thousands of fighters to the Afghan jihad, and its ideology spawned the most virulent Islamist terrorist groups such as the Jama'a Islamiyya and the Egyptian Jihad. Qaradawi is also the Director of the European Council for Fatwa and Research, part of the Muslim Brotherhood's vast European network that works for the Islamization of European societies and their domination by Islam. Qaradawi has justified Palestinian suicide bombings of Israeli civilians as compliant with shari'a.

The Deputy Chairman of the European Council for Fatwa and Research is the Lebanese Sheikh Faisal al-Mawlawi, who now lives in France, where he founded the Union Des Organisations Islamiques En France (UOIF), and the European College for Islamic Studies, both part of the Muslim Brotherhood network.

The links that such eminent leaders of the Islamic financial systems have with extremist organizations whose aim is the establishment of a world-wide Islamic state should give pause to those who welcome sharia-compliant banking and finance in the West.

Appendix 4
Shari'a Finance in Some Other Non-Muslim States

Singapore

Singapore is a small city-state in proximity to large Muslim states such as Malaysia and Indonesia. As a major international financial centre, it is greatly interested in getting a share of the lucrative shari'a finance market and the growing wealth of Muslim oil states. As its Senior Minister, Goh Chok Tong, explained:

> Singapore cannot be a complete international financial centre, if we do not offer Islamic financial services.[244]

Recognizing that its own Muslim market is relatively small, Singapore plans to build on its existing financial infrastructure to add financial products and services that can then be offered for wholesale market activities. It is encouraging its financial institutions to add Islamic products and services as well as encouraging Islamic financial institutions to open branches in Singapore.[245] By 2007 eleven Middle Eastern banks had set up operations in Singapore. Singapore is also encouraging the holding of conferences on shari'a finance in Singapore, such as the International Waqf Conference 2007 (held on 6 March 2007).[246]

Hong Kong

In October 2007, Hong Kong's Chief Executive, Donald Tsang, expressed his desire for Hong Kong to emulate Singapore and Malaysia in becoming a centre for shari'a finance. He explained that the provision of shari'a-compliant products offers huge potential for development. He stated that Hong Kong would focus on developing an Islamic bond market, as well as offering financial services to Islamic states.[247]

Japan

Japan is a latecomer to shari'a finance. However, in 2006 Mitsubishi UFJ (Japan's largest bank) forged an alliance with Malaysia's CIMB Group to provide Islamic investment banking services. In September 2007 its Central Bank, the Bank of Japan, decided to join the Islamic Financial Services Board (IFSB) as an observer in order to deepen its knowledge of shari'a finance. Also in September 2007, the first real-estate transaction compliant with Islamic law was signed in Japan: the asset manager Atlas Partners Japan in partnership with Kuwait's Boubayan Bank signed a deal to buy three office buildings in Tokyo worth $40 million.[248]

Sri Lanka

In Sri Lanka, the state-owned Bank of Ceylon planned to open Islamic banking operations in 2008. By 2007 the Sri Lanka shari'a finance sector was only $45 million, but its potential was estimated at $700-900 million.[249]

Appendix 5
Shari'a

Introduction

Shari'a is an Arabic word meaning "path" or "way". Nowadays it is used to mean "Islamic law", the detailed system of religious law developed by Muslim scholars in the first three centuries of Islam. This law expresses the Islamic way of life. Shari'a covers all aspects of life and does not separate the secular sphere from the religious sphere.

Most Muslims hold that shari'a protects them from sin like a fence or a roadblock. It also serves as an identity marker separating Muslims from non-Muslims. Shari'a strongly influences the behavior and worldview of most Muslims, even in secular states where it forms no part of the law of the land.

Most Muslims believe that shari'a, as God's revealed law, perfect and eternal, is binding on individuals, society and state in all its details. They therefore believe that any criticism of shari'a is heresy. Most Sunni Muslims believe it to be completely unchangeable, although Shi'as allow for the possibility of interpreting and adapting it to new circumstances. Muslims who deny the validity of shari'a or criticize it in any way are labelled as non-Muslims (infidels or apostates) by traditionalists and Islamists. As such they face the threat of being prosecuted as apostates, a crime that carries the death penalty in shari'a.

Development and characteristics of shari'a

Shari'a is a complex legal system derived from the Islamic source texts, the Qur'an and *hadith* (traditions recording Muhammad's words and deeds), through interpretation, commentary and case law. It was created in a context in which Muslims held political power, and thus lacks guidance for Muslims living as a minority under non-Muslims.

Shari'a tries to describe in detail all possible human acts, dividing them into permitted (*halal*) and prohibited (*haram*). It subdivides them into various degrees of good or evil such as obligatory, recommended, neutral, objectionable or forbidden. It is a vast compendium of rules, regulating in detail all matters of devotional life, worship, ritual purity, marriage and inheritance, criminal offences, commerce and personal conduct down to minute details of behavior. It also regulates the governing of the Islamic state and its relationship to non-Muslims within the state as well as to enemies outside the state.

Four Sunni orthodox schools of law developed and were codified by the end of the tenth century. The work of the founders was continued by their disciples, and over the centuries several widely accepted handbooks of law were composed by famous scholars which supposedly laid down all that was needed to be known about the law for all generations.

Legal and scholastic experts interpret and apply shari'a by looking at the relevant Qur'an and *hadith* texts filtered through the long history of legal precedents, handbooks and commentaries. Modern Muslim jurists often differentiate between shari'a, the revealed divine law, and *fiqh*, the jurists' interpretation of shari'a.

Since the nineteenth century there have been efforts at reforming shari'a in a liberal direction in order to accommodate it to the modern world. Many reformers downgraded the authority of the four legal schools and of later traditions and made the good of the community (*maslaha*) their ultimate guiding principle. They stressed the importance of reason, and differentiated between a core of universal values in shari'a (which was unchangeable and eternal) and the larger part dealing with social relations (which was open to change and adaptation to new contexts).

In the contemporary Muslim world, however, it is the traditionalists and especially the Islamists, upholders of the traditional view of shari'a, who are dominating Muslim public opinion. This leaves liberal reformers as a small minority surviving mainly in the West. Liberal reformers face heavy pressure from Islamists and traditionalists who brand them apostates and infidels and attack them verbally, legally and physically.

Muslims often claim that shari'a was quite moderate by the standards of the seventh to tenth centuries when it was created. However it has remained unchanged since then, and is thus extremely harsh compared to modern Western standards. It infringes many modern principles of human rights, religious freedom and equality of all before the law. Shari'a inherently discriminates against women, non-Muslims and "heretical Muslims" as well as against Muslims who choose to convert to another faith.

Five main areas in which shari'a is incompatible with human rights

Hudud *punishments*

These are the severe punishments prescribed by shari'a for some offences defined as being against God himself. The punishments for these crimes are seen as divinely ordained and cannot be changed by humans. These include 100 lashes or stoning to death for adultery, 80 lashes for false accusation of adultery, amputation of limbs for theft, 40 or 80 lashes for drinking alcohol, imprisonment, amputation or death (by crucifixion in serious cases) for highway robbery, and the death penalty for apostasy from Islam.

Many Islamic scholars, academics and popular preachers support the present-day application of *hudud* punishments, seeing them as identity markers of true Islamic revival.

Jews, Christians and other non-Muslims

Discrimination on the basis of religion is fundamental to shari'a. Islam must be dominant and only Muslims are full citizens, so Muslims are treated as far superior to all others.

Jews and Christians are defined as *dhimmis* (literally "people of the pact [of protection]" i.e. permitted to live). However this protection is on condition that they do not bear arms, know their lowly place in society, treat Muslims with respect, pay a special poll tax (*jizya*), and do not behave arrogantly. Numerous petty shari'a laws are used to restrict and humiliate *dhimmis* in their daily lives.

The general attitude of contempt for non-Muslims created by centuries of applying such laws means that, even in modern secular Muslim states that have constitutionally guaranteed equal rights to all citizens, non-Muslims are discriminated against in numerous ways.

Muslim heretics and apostates

Muslims who accept teachings considered heretical by orthodox Islam are held by shari'a to have reverted to paganism and therefore to deserve the death penalty. The same is true for Muslims converting to another religion (apostates), who are considered as traitors. All schools of shari'a agree that adult male apostates from Islam should be killed. Even where the death sentence is not carried out, their marriages may be automatically dissolved and they face severe penalties such as exile, disinheritance, loss of possessions, threats, beatings, torture, and prison. Many liberal or secularist Muslims find themselves in danger of being classified as apostates for views that the religious establishment or militant Islamist groups hold to be heretical. Muslim "heretical" sects are severely persecuted.

Holy War – jihad

Shari'a lays down jihad as one of the most basic religious duties, clearly indicating by the regulations listed that jihad is understood as physical warfare. Linked to the concept of jihad is the division of the world into two opposing domains: the House of Islam (*Dar al-Islam*) and the House of War (*Dar al-Harb*). Muslims are supposed to wage jihad to change the House of War (where non-Muslims are politically dominant) into the House of Islam (politically dominated by Muslims). Although some modern Muslims reject this aggressive understanding of jihad, most Muslims agree that jihad includes defending Muslim territory and Muslims from any form of aggression; this leaves the door open to interpreting any conflict involving Muslims as a case of defensive jihad. Islamic terror groups justify their atrocities by references to the shari'a rules on jihad.

Status of women

Shari'a also discriminates on the basis of gender. Men are regarded as superior. Women are treated as deficient in intelligence, morals and religion, and must therefore be protected from their own weaknesses. Shari'a rules enforce modesty in dress and behavior and the segregation of genders. They place women under the legal guardianship of their male relatives. Women are inherently of less value than men in many legal rulings. A man is allowed up to four wives, but women can have only one husband. A man can divorce his wife easily; a woman faces great obstacles should she want to divorce her husband. A daughter inherits half as much as a son, and the testimony of a female witness in court is worth only half that of a male witness. In cases of murder, the compensation for a woman is less than that given for a man.

In many Muslim societies gender segregation in public is imposed or encouraged. Shari'a courts often display a clear gender bias. This is seen in the widespread practice of accusing rape victims of illicit sexual relations (*zina*), an offence that carries punishments ranging from imprisonment and flogging to death by stoning. The victim is thus transformed into a culprit.

Challenge of shari'a in Western countries

Shari'a poses a challenge to Western societies because of the constant pressure in Muslim communities to implement it and expand its area of influence. For many Muslims in the West, secular law lacks legitimacy, especially in the realm of family law. They claim the right as a religious minority to follow their own customs and laws, including shari'a.

Creation of a parallel alternative legal framework

Many Muslims in the West try to live by shari'a regulations as far as possible, creating an unofficial enclave in which Islamic religious scholars and lawyers offer their services. This has created an alternative legal structure of shari'a courts and councils.

The stronger the parallel network of Islamic institutions becomes, the more pressure is exerted on Muslims to use these in preference to non-Muslim institutions. Once a shari'a alternative is available, it becomes obligatory for Muslims to obey shari'a in that specific case. Many Muslim leaders are constantly applying pressure on Western society, institutions and legal systems to adapt as far as possible to Muslim shari'a concepts and models, while at the same time constructing their own alternative shari'a systems.

In September 2008 it was revealed that four shari'a courts had already been operating in Britain for more than a year. By classifying themselves as arbitration tribunals they ensure that their rulings are enforceable through the secular courts.[250]

Marriage and divorce

Women are undoubtedly the main victims of the shari'a system, which inherently favors the husband. For instance, it is very common, even for well-educated Muslims, to think it unnecessary to register their marriages in British civil law. Some wrongly believe that the Islamic wedding ceremony is recognized by British law. In cases of divorce the women are then left with the much lesser legal rights of a "cohabitee".

Child marriages

In several Muslim countries child marriages are legal. For many traditional Muslims, child marriages are acceptable because Muhammad married his favorite wife Aisha when she was six years old and consummated the marriage when she was nine. Even in Britain it is possible that child marriages are happening.

Polygamy

Under shari'a a man is allowed up to four wives. Polygamy is allowed in many Muslim countries but prohibited in Western countries. This raises problems of Muslim residents in the West who married another wife either before their immigration or while visiting their "home countries".

Female genital mutilation (FGM)

Female genital mutilation is widespread among some Muslim communities, especially in Egypt, East Africa, Yemen, and Indonesia. Some Muslim leaders condemn it as un-Islamic, but many believe that it is ordained in the shari'a. They also believe it is essential for preserving women's chastity, on which the all-important family honor largely depends. In 1994 the former Sheikh of Al-Azhar, Egypt, Jad Al-Haqq 'Ali Jad Al-Haqq, ruled that circumcision is an Islamic duty for women as well as for men. In the UK it is a criminal offence under the 1985 Prohibition of Female Circumcision Act, but an estimated 7,000 girls in Britain are of an age to be at risk from this procedure at any given time.

Veiling

In shari'a there are differences between the various schools of law as to how much a woman may reveal in public. It would seem that the majority of classical scholars agreed that a woman's face may be displayed, and a minority said the face must be covered. Practice thus differed regionally depending on which school of law was followed in that area. Both Qur'an and *hadith* urge modesty in women's dress and command them to cover themselves in public. The problem is a matter of interpretation of the original Arabic words used.

Some modern Muslim women in the West are adopting the strictest version as a way of asserting their Muslim identity. It appears that Muslim organizations in the West are manipulating the issue to further the Islamization of their host societies. The problem of full veiling of the face for security and anti-terrorist measures is obvious.

Halal *products*

According to shari'a, certain foods such as pork and alcohol are forbidden to Muslims. The shari'a also says that animals must be slaughtered by Muslims in a religious ritual which includes slitting the animal's throat and draining its blood. Stunning of animals before slaughter is forbidden. Only meat produced by this type of slaughter is *halal* (permitted) for consumption. *Halal* food is provided in many public institutions in the UK such as schools, hospitals and prisons. This trend can be seen as part of a process of Islamization, whereby non-Muslims end up living by Islamic rules.

Though the Qur'an specifically prohibits only pork and alcohol, the Islamic Food and Nutrition Council of America has made a list of 36 different categories of food, drinks, and cosmetic products covering 301 products that meet shari'a requirements. Such products must not contain any prohibited ingredients and must be processed according to Islamic guidelines.

Shari'a principles used to allow the existence of Muslim minorities in the West

Under the traditional division of the world into the House of Islam and the House of War, Muslim scholars recommended that Muslims who found themselves under non-Muslim rule should migrate back to Muslim states so that it would be easier for them to live according to shari'a. Today, most scholars accept the validity of Muslims living in the West under non-Islamic rule, but grapple with the legal justifications and implications of this situation.

Some Muslim leaders in the West make obedience to the law of the land conditional on such laws not contradicting shari'a. Some modernist scholars, however, have tried to redefine Western states as belonging to the "House of Islam" but this has been strongly opposed by most Muslims. Others have developed concepts such as defining Western states as "House of Security" (*Dar al-Aman*) or "House of Covenant"

(*Dar al-'Ahd*) to justify Muslims living in Western states and complying with non-shari'a norms.

The shari'a principle of *darura* is used by many Muslim scholars to justify Muslim minorities living in the West who adapt to Western norms, including complying with Western legal systems and being loyal to Western states. *Darura* states that in emergency circumstances that threaten the life and welfare of Muslims, the unlawful may become lawful (necessity lifts prohibition), thus allowing Muslims in a non-Muslim state to disregard shari'a rules that conflict with the law of the land.

Other legal tools employed include the notion of public good (*maslaha*) and the permission to use suitable rulings from any of the schools of law rather than being limited to one's own school of law.

While these are all useful tools for moderate Muslims to justify their living in non-Muslim societies, they are generally considered merely temporary, applicable only in times of Muslim weakness. The implication is that all good Muslims ought to struggle to change this not-ideal situation into the ideal of Muslim political domination and shari'a rule.

Further Reading

1   Doi, 'Abdur Rahman, *Shari'ah: The Islamic Law*. Kuala Lumpur: A.S. Noordeen, 1984.

2   Al-Qaradawi, Yusuf, *The Lawful and the Prohibited in Islam*. Indianapolis, Indiana: American Trust Publications, no date.

3   *Shari'a and Muslims in the West*. Barnabas Fund, 2007.

Endnotes

1   Brian Hanney, "Shari'a and the City," *accountancy magazine*, May 2008, pp23-24.

2   "Qatar Islamic Expects UK Bank License in Weeks," Asharq al-Awsat, November 25, 2007, http://www.asharq-e.com/news.asp?section=6&id=10983.

3   Ali Parsa, "Shariah property investment: developing an international strategy." London: Royal Institution of Chartered Surveyors, 2005.

4   Natasha De Teran, "Islamic Finance in London: The City Makes a Head Start for Hub Status," *The Banker*, September 1, 2007, http://www.accessmylibrary.com/coms2/summary_0286-32852686_ITM (viewed 29 October 2007).

5   Dogu Ergil, "Is there an Islamic economy?" *Todays Zaman*, October 17, 2007, http://www.todayszaman.com/tz-web/yazarDetay.do?haberno=124757 (viewed October 26, 2007).

6   Tina Nielsen, "Banking on Islamic Finance", Director, April 2008.

7   See for example "subsection 4: Economically [The Economic Organization] of section Five: Comprehensive Settlement Organization" in *An Explanatory Memorandum On the General Strategic Goal for the Group In North America 5/22/1991*, http://www.investigativeproject.org/documents/misc/20.pdf. See also the "Articles of Agreement" of the Islamic Development Bank, http://www.isdb.org/irj/portal/anonymous?NavigationTarget=navurl://a9ce3372c713aae67502ee72086da289.

8   Zamir Iqbal & Abbas Mirakhor, *An Introduction To Islamic Finance: Theory And Practice*. London: John Wiley & Sons, 2007, p17. Quoted in "Islamic Finance: Origins, Emergence, and Future," *The Illinois Business Law Journal*, 18 September 2007, http://ibisjournal.typepad.com/Illinois_business_law_soc/2007/09/Islamic-finance.html (viewed June 10, 2008).

9   Caroline B. Glick, "Shari'a-friendly investments," *Jewish World Review*, October 23, 2007.

10 Ergil, "Is there an Islamic economy?"

11 *Hadith* are traditions that record what Muhammad and his early followers said and did. Some are considered more authentic and reliable than others, but in general the *hadith* are considered second in importance only to the Qur'an itself as a source of guidance for Muslims.

12 Nes'et Cagatay, "Riba and Interest Concept and Banking in the Ottoman Empire," *Studia Islamica*, No. 32, 1970, p57.

13 Mustafa Akyol, "Is capitalism compatible with Islam?" *The Turkish Daily News*, February 19, 2007.

14 Akyol, "Is capitalism compatible with Islam?"

15 M. Siddieq Noorzoy, "Islamic Laws on riba (Interest) and Their Economic Implications," *International Journal of Middle East Studies*, Vol. 14: No.1, February 1982, p8.

16 Nes'et Cagatay, p63, citing Kapu Kulu Ocalari by Ismail Hakki Uzuncarsili, 1, p254.

17 Mustafa Akyol, "Is capitalism compatible with Islam?"

18 Ibrahim Halebi, Multaka al Abhur. Transl. M. Mevkufati. 1890; Mehmet b. Hurmuz (alias Mullah Husrav), Tarcama-i Durar. 1842. These are Fiqh books used as text books in Ottoman *madrasas*. These texts discuss *riba*.

19 Nes'et Cagatay, "Riba and Interest Concept and Banking in the Ottoman Empire," p56.

20 Nes'et Cagatay, "Riba and Interest Concept and Banking in the Ottoman Empire," p58.

21 Fatawa'i Fayzia, 1, p43, cited in Nes'et Cagatay.

22 Nes'et Cagatay, "Riba and Interest Concept and Banking in the Ottoman Empire," p65.

23 Nes'et Cagatay, "Riba and Interest Concept and Banking in the Ottoman Empire," p68.

24 Timur Kuran, *Islam & Mammon: The Economic Predicaments of Islamism*. Princeton, NJ: Princeton University Press, 2004, pp2-3, 38, 84-89.

25 Abul A'la Mawdudi, *Jihad fi Sabilillah*. Transl. by Prof. Khurshid Ahmad. Edited by Huda Khattab. Birmingham: UKIM Dawah Centre, 1997, ch4.

26 Hassan Al-Banna, *Five Tracts of Hassan al-Banna (1906–1949): A Selection From the Majmu at Rasa'il al-Imam al-Shahid*. Berkeley, CA: University of California Press, 1978, pp24, 71-72.

27 Khurram Murad, "Introduction," in Abul A la Mawdudi, *The Islamic Movement: Dynamics of Values, Power and Change*. Leicester: The Islamic Foundation, 1984, pp11-12.

28 Isma il Raji al-Faruqi, *Islam*. Beltsville, MD: Amana Publications, 1985, p65.

Endnotes

29   Khurshid Ahmad, "Introduction" in Khurshid Ahmad ed., *Studies in Islamic Economics*. Leicester: The Islamic Foundation, 1980, ppxiii-xiv.

30   Khurshid Ahmad, "Economic Development in an Islamic Framework," in Khurshid Ahmad (ed.), *Studies in Islamic Economics*, pp182, 188.

31   Translated from the Arabic. See http://www.elaph.com/elaphWeb/politics/2008/1/294647.htm.

32   Dr. Muhammad Muhsin Khan and Dr. Muhammad Taqi-ud-Din Al-Hilali, *Interpretation of the Meanings of the Noble Qur'an in the English Language*, revised edition. Riyadh: Darussalam Publishers and Distributors, February 2001.

33   Khan and Al-Hilali, *Interpretation of the Meanings of the Noble Qur'an in the English Language*.

34   Nes'et Cagatay , "Riba and Interest Concept and Banking in the Ottoman Empire," p54; Timur Kuran, "Interest," in John L. Esposito (ed.), *The Oxford Encyclopedia of the Modern Islamic World*, Vol. 2. New York: Oxford University Press, 1995, pp205-207.

35   Timur Kuran, *Islam & Mammon: The Economic Predicaments of Islamism*, pp14-16.

36   A. Yusuf Ali, *The Holy Qur'an: Text, Translation and Commentary*. Leicester: The Islamic Foundation, 1975.

37   Note 324 to Q 2:275, A. Yusuf Ali, *The Holy Qur'an: Text, Translation and Commentary*, p111.

38   "Islamic institute blesses interest," BBC News, November 18, 2002.

39   Ibrahim Warde, *Islamic Finance in the Global Economy*. Edinburgh: Edinburgh University Press, 2001, pp56-57. See also Timur Kuran, "Interest."

40   Ibrahim Warde, *Islamic Finance in the Global Economy*, pp56-58.

41   Mohammed Khalil, "Q & A with the Grand Mufti of Egypt," Asharq Alawsat, July 14, 2007.

42   "Sheikh Alazhar: The banks' interest rate is lawful according to the Islamic law," *Alaswaq*, October 2, 2007, http://www.alaswaq.net/articles/2007/10/02/11204.html (viewed October 26, 2007).

43   Timur Kuran, "Interest," pp. 205-207.

44   Dr. Muhammad Saleem, *Islamic Banking: A Charade; Call For Enlightenment*. BookSurge, LLC, 2006, p1.

45   M. Siddieq Noorzoy, "Islamic Laws on Riba (Interest) and their Economic Implications," *International Journal of Middle East Studies*, Vol. 14: Issue 1, 1982, pp3-17.

46   Seyyed Vali Reza Nasr, "Islamic Economics: Novel Perspectives," in Tim Niblock & Rodney Wilson (eds.), *The Political Economy of the Middle East, Volume III: Islamic Economics*. Cheltenham & Northampton, MA: Edward Elgar Publishing, pp205-219.

47   Mohamed Ariff, "Islamic Banking," *Asian-Pacific Economic Literature*, Vol. 2: No. 2, September 1988, pp46-62.

48   Mahmoud Amin El-Gamal, "Overview of Islamic Finance," US Department of the Treasury, Office of International Affairs, Occasional paper No. 4, August 2006.

49   Seyyed Vali Reza Nasr, "Islamic Economics: Novel Perspectives."

50   Clement M. Henry and Rodney Wilson (eds.), *The Politics of Islamic Finance*. Edinburgh: Edinburgh University Press, 2004, p8.

51   Resolutions of the Securities Commission Shariah Advisory Council, 2nd ed. Kuala Lumpur: Securities Commission, 2007, pp96-98.

52   Galal Fakkar, "Plans to Establish World Fund for Zakah," *Arab News*, October 26, 2007.

53   Galal Fakkar, "Plans to Establish World Fund for Zakah."

54   *Tafsir Ibn Kathir* (Abridged). Vol. 4. Riyadh: Darussalam, 2003, p. 458.

55   "Faith, Hate and Charity," Panorama, BBC1, July 30, 2006, http://www.bbc. co.uk/pressoffice/pressreleases/stories/2006/07_july/30/panorama.shtml.

56   Nimrod Raphaeli, "Islamic Banking – A Fast Growing Industry," *MEMRI, Inquiry and Analysis Series*, No. 297, September 29, 2006.

57   Timur Kuran, "The Religious Undercurrents Of Muslim Economic Grievances," *Social Science Research Council (SSRC)*, http://www.ssrc.org/sept11/essays/kuran. htm (viewed October 29, 2007).

58   Mahmoud A. El-Gamal, "Limits and Dangers of Shari'a Arbitrage," www.ruf.rice. edu/~elgamal/files/Arbitrage.pdf (viewed June 17, 2008).

59   El-Gamal, "Limits and Dangers of Shari'a Arbitrage," http://www.nubank.com/ islamic/index.html.

60   Mahmoud A. El-Gamal, "'Interest' and the Paradox of Contemporary Islamic Law and Finance," http://www.ruf.rice.edu/~elgamal/files/interest.pdf (viewed June 13, 2008).

61   Mahmoud A. El-Gamal, "Money Laundering and Terror Financing Issues in the Middle East," prepared statement for US Senate Committee on Banking, Housing and Urban Affairs hearing, July 13, 2005, http://www.ruf.rice.edu/~elgamal/files/ Testimony.pdf (viewed June 17, 2008).

62   Timur Kuran, "The Genesis of Islamic Economics: A Chapter in the Politics of Muslim Identity," Social Research, Vol. 64: no. 2, Summer 1997, http://www. mtholyoke.edu/acad/intrel/kuran.htm.

63   Kuran, *Islam & Mammon: The Economic Predicaments of Islamism,* pp16-17.

64   Dogu Ergil, "Is there an Islamic economy?" http://www.todayszaman.com/tz-web/ yazarDetay.do?haberno=124757 (viewed October 26, 2007).

Endnotes

65   Kuran, *Islam & Mammon: The Economic Predicaments of Islamism*, pp. 43-44.

66   "Public being looted in name of Islamic banking: expert," *Pakistan Press International (PPI)*, November 2006, http://www.accessmylibrary.com/coms2/summary_0286-26928086_ITM (viewed October 29, 2007).

67   Dr. Muhammad Saleem, *Islamic Banking: A Charade; Call For Enlightenment*, p41

68   Muhammad Saleem, "Islamic Banking A 300 Billion Deception," Xlibris Corporation, USA, 2005.

69   Saleem "Islamic Banking," p56.

70   "Setting the benchmarks", *Executive Magazine*, 15 June 2008.

71   Quoted in "Islamic banking 'approaching a crossroad'", http://www.zawya.com/marketing.cfm?zp&p=/story.cfm?id=ZAWYA20040225134523.

72   Kuran, *Islam & Mammon: The Economic Predicaments of Islamism*, pp52-54, 60-61.

73   Kuran, *Islam & Mammon: The Economic Predicaments of Islamism*, p39.

74   Mahmoud Amin El-Gamal, "Overview of Islamic Finance," US Department of the Treasury, Office of International Affairs, Occasional paper No. 4, August 2006.

75   See for instance on its growth in Jordan and the involvement of the Muslim Brotherhood: Mohammed Malley, "The Political Implications of Islamic Finance in Jordan," University of Texas, paper prepared for the 2001 Annual Meeting of the Middle East Studies Association, San Francisco, November 17-20, 2001.

76   Mahmoud Amin El-Gamal, "Overview of Islamic Finance".

77   Kuran, *Islam & Mammon: The Economic Predicaments of Islamism*.

78   Ariff, "Islamic Banking."

79   Henry and Wilson (eds.), *The Politics of Islamic Finance*, p. 5.

80   Khurshid Ahmad, "Introduction" in Khurshid Ahmad ed., *Studies in Islamic Economics*, pp.xvii-xviii.

81   Translated from the Arabic, http://www.alaswaq.net/articles/2008/01/22/13481.html

82   Mohammad Hashim Kamali, "Islamic banking and jurisprudence: nit-picking or seeing the bigger picture?" *New Horizon*, Issue No. 166, October-November 2007, pp12-13.

83   Islamic Fiqh Council, Mecca, 1985, quoted in Mahmoud Amin El Gamal, *A Basic Guide to Contemporary Islamic Banking and Finance*. Rice University, June 2000, p31, http://www.witness-pioneer.org/vil/Books/MG_CIBF/chapter_5.htm (viewed August 8, 2008).

84   Mahmoud Amin El-Gamal, "A Basic Guide to Contemporary Islamic Banking and Finance."

85   Muhammad bin Salih al-'Uthaimin, *Al-sharh Al-mumti' 'ala Zad Al-mustaqni'*, Vol.8. Cairo: Almaktaba Altawfiqiah, n.d., pp2-3.

86   http://www.usc.edu/dept/MSA/fundamentals/hadithsunnah/abudawud/014.sat.html#014.2498.

87   See for example, Dr. Muhammad Saleem, *Islamic Banking: A Charade; Call For Enlightenment*, pp89-91. For more on the working concept of "functional equivalence," see the OCC Interpretive Letter #806, December 1997, 12 U.S.C. 24 (7), 12 U.S.C. 371, p4, http://www.occ.treas.gov/interp/dec97/int806.pdf .

88   "A financial jihad", *Al-Ahram Weekly*, Issue 613, November 21-27, 2002.

89   "A financial jihad".

90   "Visionary, who nurtured an Asian 'tiger'", *Hindustan Times*, November 17-18, 2006, http://www.hindustantimes.com/news/specials/leadership2006/ht_091106.shtml.

91   Posting of FBIS Translated Text of December 27, 2001 statement by Osama bin Laden (carried on Al-Jazirah Satellite Channel Television), http://groups.yahoo.com/group/MewNews/message/4339 (viewed June 17, 2008).

92   "A financial jihad."

93   See for instance David Leigh and Rob Evans, "Britain 'powerless to resist Saudi threats'," *Guardian Weekly*, February 22, 2008.

94   *Tafsir ibn Kathir, Abridged*, 2nd edition, vol. 2. Translated and abridged by a group of scholars under the supervision of Sheikh Safiur-Rahman Al-Mubarakpuri, Houston, Texas: Darussalam Publications, 2003, pp74-79.

95   Tafsir al-Tabari, 6:25, quoted in *Tafsir ibn Kathir, Abridged*, p79.

96   Yusuf al-Qaradawi, *The Lawful and the Prohibited in Islam*. Plainfield, Indiana: American Trust Publications, 1994, p264.

97   El-Gamal, "A Basic Guide to Contemporary Islamic Banking and Finance," p4, http://www.nubank.com/islamic/index.html (viewed 27 May 2008).

98   El-Gamal, "A Basic Guide to Contemporary Islamic Banking and Finance," p4, http://www.nubank.com/islamic/index.html (viewed May 27, 2008).

99   Gal Luft, "Oil and the New Economic Order," Insitute for the Analysis of Global Security (IAGS), February 2008, p6, http://www.iags.org/new_economic_order0208.pdf.

100   Posting of FBIS Translated Text of December 27, 2001 statement by Osama bin Laden.

101   Gal Luft, "Oil and the New Economic Order," Insitute for the Analysis of Global Security (IAGS), February 2008, pp6, 11, http://www.iags.org/new_economic_order0208.pdf (viewed June 18, 2008).

102   Abul A'la Mawdudi, *Jihad fi Sabilillah*, chapter 2.

103   Abul A'la Mawdudi, *Jihad fi Sabilillah*, p22 and chapter 3.

104   See for examples: re: legal: the OCC's Interpretive Letter #867, November 1999, 12 USC 24(7), 12 USC 29; or media: *Ibid* 11, and numerous others.

105   It is astonishing that so many in the Western media, governments, etc. who discuss Islamic finance matter-of-factly as a well-defined and understood, uniformly-held

religious obligation mandated by shariʻa law will at the same time ignore or deny shariʻaʼs clear rulings and decisive authority on other matters such as apostasy, jihad, and the status of women and non-Muslims.

106 *Resolutions of the Securities Commission Shariah Advisory Council*, 2nd edition. Kuala Lumpur: Securities Commission, 2007, pp96-98.

107 "Tarek Fatah, "Banks are helping Sharia make a back door entrance," *The Globe and Mail*, January 25, 2008.

108 El-Din, "A financial jihad."

109 Nicholas Ridley, "The development of Islamic banking and financial institutions, and potential vulnerabilities to criminal exploitation and terrorist fund transfers," John Grieve Center for Police Studies, London Metropolitan University, November 2007, p3.

110 El-Din, "A Financial Jihad."

111 Yiagadeesen Samy, "Terrorism Financing and Financial System Vulnerabilities: Issues and Challenges," Canadian Centre for Intelligence and Security Studies: Trends in Terrorism Series, Vol. 2006-3, http://www.csis-scrs.gc.ca/en/itac/itac-docs/2006-3.asp.

112 Jean-Charles Brisard, "Terrorism Financing: Roots and trends of Saudi terrorism financing," report prepared for the President of the Security Council, United Nations, December 19, 2002, p3, http://www.investigativeproject.org/documents/testimony/22.pdf (viewed June 18, 2008).

113 Mahmoud A. El-Gamal, "Limits and Dangers of Shariʻa Arbitrage," http://www.ruf.rice.edu/~elgamal/files/arbitrage.pdf (viewed June 13, 2008).

114 Mahmoud A. El-Gamal, "Money Laundering and Terror Financing Issues in the Middle East," statement for US Senate Committee on Banking, Housing and Urban Affairs hearing,, July 13, 2005, http://www.ruf.rice.edu/~elgamal/files/Testimony.pdf (viewed 13 June 2008).

115 El-Gamal, "Overview of Islamic Finance."

116 El-Din, "A financial jihad."

117 El-Din, "A financial jihad."

118 Accounting and Auditing Organization for Islamic Financial Institutions.

119 El-Din, "A financial jihad."

120 "Search for Islamic Scholars Increasingly Difficult with Prosperity of Islamic Banks," translated from the Arabic by MEMRI, al-Qabas, Kuwait, http://memrieconomicblog.org/bin/content.cgi?article=114.

121 "Approaches to Regulation of Islamic Financial Services Industry," Governor's Speech at the IFSB Summit – Islamic Financial Services Industry and The Global Regulatory Environment, May 18, 2004, http://www.bnm.gov.my/index.php?ch=9&pg=15&ac=151&print=1.

122 "Approaches to Regulation of Islamic Financial Services Industry."

123 El-Gamal, "Overview of Islamic Finance."

124 "Nice work if you can get it," Business Middle East, Economist Intelligence Unit, October 16, 2007.

125 Hassan Kaleem, "A scholar's viewpoint," *accountancy magazine*, May 2008, pp26-27.

126 "Nice work if you can get it."

127 Ibrahim Warde, "Islamic Finance in the Global Economy," p 227.

128 http://archive.gulfnews.com/articles/07/03/31/10114772.html .

129 Lahem al Nasser, "Shariah Standard Lists for Trading," *Asharq al-Awsat*, March 12, 2008.

130 "'Most sukuk 'not Islamic', body claims," Reuters, November 22, 2007, http://www.arabianbusiness.com/504577-most-sukuk-not-islamic-say-scholars#targetCommentForm (viewed June 18, 2008).

131 al-Nasser, "Shariah Standard Lists for Trading."

132 "Islamic Banks: A Novelty No Longer," http://www.businessweek.com/magazine/content/05_32/b3946141_mz035.htm (viewed June 18, 2008).

133 For more on this subject, see David Yerushalmi, "Shari'ah's Black Box: Civil Liability and Criminal Exposure Surrounding Shari'ah-Compliant Finance," http://papers.ssrn.com/sol3/papers.cfm?abstract_id=1101905#PaperDownload.

134 "Islamic Finance in the UK: Regulations and Challenges," Financial Services Authority, November 2007, p14, http://www.fsa.gov.uk/pubs/other/islamic_finance.pdf .

135 For more analysis of these issues from an Islamic perspective, see Muhammad Shabbir, "Adequacy of Disclosure in Islamic Financial Institutions," Institute of Islamic Banking and Insurance, http://www.islamic-banking.com/aom/ibanking/m_shabbir.php.

136 Ariff, "Islamic Banking."

137 "Gatehouse sees more UK Islamic investment banks", *Daily Times*, 13 August 2008; "Interest-free Sharia MasterCard launched", 11 August 2008, http://www.metro.co.uk/news/article.html?in_article_id=258913&in_page_id=34&ito=newsnow (viewed 17 September 2008).

138 "Islamic investment basics,", BBC News, January 24, 2002.

139 El-Gamal, "Overview of Islamic Finance."

140 Ariff, "Islamic Banking."

141 Clement and Wilson (eds.), *The Politics of Islamic Finance*, p5.

142 Osman Babikir Ahmad, "Islamic Banking In Practice," Paper Presented at the International Course On Principles And Practices Of Islamic Economics And Banking, November 2006.

Endnotes

143 El-Gamal, "Overview of Islamic Finance."

144 Rodney Wilson, "On the verge of a boom," *Islamic Banking and Finance*, No. 8.

145 Timur Kuran, "The Religious Undercurrents Of Muslim Economic grievances," *Social Science Research Council (SSRC)*, http://www.ssrc.org/sept11/essays/kuran. htm (viewed October 29, 2007).

146 Osman Babikir Ahmad, "Islamic Banking In Practice."

147 Ariff, "Islamic Banking."

148 Farhan Bokhari, "Iran's Islamic banking model faces challenges," *The Financial Times*, October 8, 2007.

149 Ridley, "The development of Islamic banking and financial institutions, and potential vulnerabilities to criminal exploitation and terrorist fund transfers," pp17-18.

150 Paul Klebnikov, "Millionaire Mullahs," *Forbes*, July 21, 2003; http://www.forbes. com/global/2003/0721/024_print.html, (viewed June 18, 2008).

151 Paul Klebnikov, "Millionaire Mullahs."

152 Paul Klebnikov, "Millionaire Mullahs."

153 Paul Klebnikov, "Millionaire Mullahs."

154 Trish Schuh, "Iranians: They're Just Like Us!" *Esquire*, March 12, 2008, http:// www.esquire.com/the-side/blog/iranians-like-us-031208 (viewed 18 June 2008).

155 Osman Babikir Ahmad, "Islamic Banking In Practice."

156 Timur Kuran, "Interest."

157 Timur Kuran, *Islam & Mammon: The Economic Predicaments of Islamism*, p57.

158 Timur Kuran, *Islam & Mammon: The Economic Predicaments of Islamism*, p57.

159 M.M. Ali, "Constitutional Changes and Prospects for Shariah Banking in Pakistan," Washington Report on Middle East Affairs, September-October 2002, p52.

160 "Islamic Banking," in State Bank of Pakistan, Annual Performance Review, 2003-2004, pp23-27.

161 El-Gamal, "Overview of Islamic Finance."

162 "Pakistan boosts rollout of Islamic banking," *Asia Pulse News*, September 13, 2007, http://www.accessmylibrary.com/coms2/summary_0286-32872430_ITM (viewed October 29, 2007).

163 Farhan Bukhari, " Islamic Finance – Promise in Pakistan," *The Banker*, January 4, 2007, http://www.accessmylibrary.com/coms2/summary_0286-30242269_ITM (viewed October 29, 2007).

164 "Islamic banking in Pak attracts foreign investments," *The Press Trust of India*, October 6, 2007, http://www.accessmylibrary.com/coms2/summary_0286-33073842_ITM (viewed October 29, 2007).

165 Osman Babikir Ahmad, "Islamic Banking In Practice."

166 Osman Babikir Ahmad, "Islamic Banking In Practice."

167 *Resolutions of the Securities Commission Shariah Advisory Council*, 2nd edition. Kuala Lumpur: Securities Commission, 2007, pp96-98.

168 "Islamic Banking Grows in Gulf," *Oxford Analytica*, September 1, 2007.

169 El-Gamal, "Overview of Islamic Finance."

170 "Islamic Banks: A Novelty No Longer", *Business Week Online*, August 8, 2005.

171 Henry and Wilson (eds.), *The Politics of Islamic Finance*, p8.

172 Ridley, "The development of Islamic banking and financial institutions, and potential vulnerabilities to criminal exploitation and terrorist fund transfers," p22.

173 Ridley, "The development of Islamic banking and financial institutions, and potential vulnerabilities to criminal exploitation and terrorist fund transfers," p23.

174 El-Gamal, "Overview of Islamic Finance."

175 Rodney Wilson, "On the verge of a boom."

176 Henry and Wilson (eds.), *The Politics of Islamic Finance*, p8.

177 "Islamic Banking Grows in Gulf."

178 Craig Nethercott, Mohammed Al Sheikh, et al., "Islamic Project Finance in the Kingdom of Saudi Arabia," *Islamic Finance News*, July 2006, http://www.islamicfinancenews.com/legalguide/articlewhitecase.php (viewed October 24, 2007).

179 See: "Saudi finance will go Islamic in five years," *Alaswaq*, January 22, 2008, http://www.alaswaq.net/articles/2008/01/22/13481.html (viewed 18 June 2008).

180 Henry and Wilson (eds.), *The Politics of Islamic Finance*, p8.

181 El-Gamal, "Overview of Islamic Finance."

182 "Islamic banking boost for Bahrain economy," *Asia Pulse News*, February 19, 2007, http://www.accessmylibrary.com/coms2/summary_0286-29674370_ITM (viewed October 29, 2007).

183 Ridley, "The development of Islamic banking and financial institutions, and potential vulnerabilities to criminal exploitation and terrorist fund transfers," p16.

184 "Islamic banking boost for Bahrain economy."

185 Ridley, "The development of Islamic banking and financial institutions, and potential vulnerabilities to criminal exploitation and terrorist fund transfers," p17.

186 Nimrod Raphaeli, "Islamic Banking – A fast Growing Industry," *MEMRI, Inquiry and Analysis Series*, No. 297, September 29, 2006.

187 Ridley, "The development of Islamic banking and financial institutions, and potential vulnerabilities to criminal exploitation and terrorist fund transfers," p17.

188 "Islamic banking solutions," *World Finance*, August-September 2007, pp50-51.

189 Ridley, "The development of Islamic banking and financial institutions, and potential vulnerabilities to criminal exploitation and terrorist fund transfers", p17.

Endnotes

190   "Muscat says no to Islamic banking: Oman ignores growth in sharia sector," *Middle East Economic Digest (MEED)*, February 16, 2007, http://www.accessmyli-brary.com/coms2/summary_0286-30069342_ITM (viewed October 29, 2007).

191   Ridley, "The development of Islamic banking and financial institutions, and potential vulnerabilities to criminal exploitation and terrorist fund transfers," p17.

192   Ridley, "The development of Islamic banking and financial institutions, and potential vulnerabilities to criminal exploitation and terrorist fund transfers," p17.

193   Osman Babikir Ahmad, "Islamic Banking In Practice."

194   Henry and Wilson (eds.), *The Politics of Islamic Finance*, p8.

195   "Islamic institute blesses interest," BBC News, 18 November 2002.

196   Ibrahim Warde, *Islamic Finance in the Global Economy*, pp56-57. See also Kuran, "Interest."

197   Ibrahim Warde, *Islamic Finance in the Global Economy*, pp56-58.

198   Henry and Wilson (eds), *The Politics of Islamic Finance*, p8.

199   El-Gamal, "Overview of Islamic Finance."

200   Ahmad, "Islamic Banking In Practice."

201   Henry and Wilson (eds.), *The Politics of Islamic Finance*, p8.

202   "Syria," International Religious Freedom Report, U.S. Department of State, 2007, released by the Bureau of Democracy, Human Rights, and Labor, http://www.state.gov/g/drl/rls/irf/2007/90221.htm (viewed August 1, 2008).

203   Ridley, "The development of Islamic banking and financial institutions, and potential vulnerabilities to criminal exploitation and terrorist fund transfers," p20.

204   Henry and Wilson (eds.), *The Politics of Islamic Finance*, p8.

205   "Mortgage and Islamic ethics: Report from European Council for Fatwa and Research," The *Bohra Chronicle*, March 2001.

206   "Mortgage and Islamic ethics: Report from European Council for Fatwa and Research."

207   El-Gamal, "Overview of Islamic Finance."

208   Ariff, "Islamic Banking."

209   Nimrod Raphaeli, "Islamic Banking – A Fast Growing Industry."

210   OCC Interpretive Letter #806, Dec. 1997, 12 U.S.C. 24 (7); OCC Interpretive Letter #867, Nov. 1999, 12 U.S.C. 24 (7) 12 U.S.C. 29.

211   See Devon Bank's Availability chart: http://www.devonbank.com/islamic/availability.html.

212   Umar F. Moghul, "Introduction to Islamic Finance," *Communities & Banking*, Summer 2006.

213   "Sheikh Dr. Yusuf Al-Qaradawi and Others: Documented Shari'aa – Jurisprudence – Opinions," http://www.lariba.com/dev/fatwas/qaradawi.htm (viewed June 18,

2008); "Sheikh Muhammad Taqi Usmani: Documented Shari'aa – Jurisprudence – Opinions," http://www.lariba.com/dev/fatwas/usmani.htm (viewed June 18, 2008).

214 "Treasury Department Appoints Islamic Finance Adviser," Bureau of International Information Programs, US Department of State, June 2, 2004, http://usinfo.state. gov/xarchives/display.html?p=washfile-english&y=2004&m=June&x=2004060218 0450ndyblehs0.2986959 (viewed October 26, 2007).

215 See Project Overview, Islamic Finance Project, Harvard Law School, http://ifptest. law.harvard.edu/ifphtml/index.php?module=about (viewed 18 June 2008).

216 Raphaeli, "Islamic Banking – A Fast Growing Industry."

217 Abdulkader Thomas, "Methods of Islamic Home Finance in the United States; beneficial breakthroughs," *The American Journal of Islamic Finance*. (Mr. Thomas is a member of the management committee of Guidance Financial Group, LLC, reportedly the largest Islamic financer of home mortgages in the US.)

218 "Muslims torn between belief and finance," *The Observer*, June 18, 2000; "Banking on the common good," *The Guardian*, June 18, 2002.

219 Julian Knight, "Non-Muslims snap up Islamic accounts," BBC News, December 17, 2006.

220 Polly Curtis, "Costing Religion," *The Guardian*, July 22, 2003; Graham Norwood, "The housing boom that forgot Muslims," *The Observer*, June 16, 2002; "Muslims tackle mortgage hurdles," BBC News, October 16, 2002.

221 "Muslim mortgages,", HSBC, *Your Money*, Issue 33, November 2003.

222 "Muslim mortgages."

223 "HSBC: Islamic mortgages attract interest," *Yahoo! Finance Commentary*, July 2, 2002; Nicola Woolcock, "No interest – but a surefire, best-selling hit," *The Daily Telegraph: Telegraph Property*, November 15, 2003. The change in the rules was announced by the Chancellor Gordon Brown in the Finance Bill in April 2003 and took effect from December 1, 2003.

224 "Islamic Finance in the UK," *Islamic Finance Home*, December 19, 2003.

225 De Teran, "Islamic Finance in London: The City Makes a Head Start for Hub Status."

226 "Islamic Banking Grows in Gulf."

227 "Speech by the Chief Secretary to the Treasury, Stephen Timms MP, at the Islamic Finance and Trade Conference," HM Treasury, June 13, 2006, http://hm-treasury. gov.uk/newsroom_and_speeches/speeches/chiefsecspeeches/speech_cst_130606. cfm (viewed October 26, 2007).

228 "UK's Brown backs Islamic finance," BBC News, June 13, 2006.

229 Abul Taher and David Smith, "Brown to boost Islamic banking," *The Sunday Times*, March 12, 2006.

230 Zahida Aslam, "London – Key Center for Islamic Finance," *Hardman & Co*, July

13, 2006, http://www.hardmanandco.com/Research/Islamic_Finance_Jul06.pdf (viewed October 26, 2007); De Teran, "Islamic Finance in London: The City Makes a Head Start for Hub Status."

231 De Teran, "Islamic Finance in London: The City Makes a Head Start for Hub Status."

232 "First Islamic stockbroking service launched," BBC News, July 28, 2003; "High Street bank offers Islamic mortgage," BBC News, July 1, 2003; Woolcock, "No interest – but a surefire, best-selling hit;" "Islamic mortgages 'worth billions', " BBC News, November 29, 2002; Liz Loxton, "Billion-pound UK market," section on "Islamic Banking," *The Times*, October 8, 2003.

233 Raphaeli, "Islamic Banking – A fast-growing Industry."

234 "Bank of London and the Middle East launches as London based Islamic bank," AME info, July 9, 2007, http://www.ameinfo.com/126027.html (viewed October 31, 2007).

235 "HSBC Amanah Global Properties Income Fund," Fund Fact Sheet, September 2002; "HSBC Amanah Financing: financing in accordance with Shariah," issued by HSBC Bank plc, Hemel Hempstead; "Our Shari'a Board," http://www.iibu.com/shariaa_board/sboard.htm.

236 "HSBC Amanah Global Properties Income Fund;" "HSBC Amanah Financing: financing in accordance with Shariah;" "Our Shari'a Board."

237 "Islamic Banking."

238 "System of divine Guidance" in "Islamic Banking."

239 De Teran, "Islamic Finance in London: The City Makes a Head Start for Hub Status."

240 Humayon A. Dar, "Demand for Islamic Financial Services in the UK: Chasing a Mirage?" Loughborough University, 2004, http://www.lboro.ac.uk/departments/ec/Reasearchpapers/2004/TSIJ.pdf (viewed October 31, 2007).

241 Ali Parsa, *Shariah property investment: developing an international strategy.* London: Royal Institution of Chartered Surveyors, 2005.

242 Islamic Bank of Britain, Annual Report and Financial Statements, December 31, 2006, p6.

243 "Lloyds TSB brings Islamic banking to Dewsbury," April 7, 2005, http://www.mediacenter.lloydstsb.com/media/pdf_irmc/mc/press_releases/2005/april/dewsbury_islamic_financial_services.pdf (viewed 31 October 2007).

244 Ong Chong Tee, "Singapore's Perspective on Islamic Finance," Opening Keynote Address, Asian Banker Summit 2005, Monetary Authority of Singapore, March 16, 2005, http://www.mas.gov.sg/news_room/statements/2005/Opening_Keynote_Address_by_DMD_Ong_at_the_Asian_Su.html (viewed July 28, 2008).

245 Tee, "Singapore's Perspective on Islamic Finance."

246 "Speech by Mr Goh Chok Tong, Senior Minister of the Republic of Singapore, at the Opening Ceremony of the Singapore International Waqf Conference

2007," Monetary Authority of Singapore, March 6, 2007, http://www.mas.gov.sg/
news_room/statements/2007/SM_Speech_International_Conference_Waqf.html
(viewed 28 July 2008).

247 Hong Kong Aims to Become Islamic Finance Hub: Tsang," *Arab News*, October 11, 2007.

248 "Japan Developing Yen for Islamic Finance," *Forbes*, November 20, 2007.

249 Kamali, "Islamic banking and jurisprudence: nit-picking or seeing the bigger picture?" p6.

250 "Revealed: UK's first official sharia courts," *The Times*, 14 September 2008.